"Rivera artfully weaves real-life stories with the Living Word. Her love for Jesus and people shines through as she uses relatable examples from daily life to illustrate God's desire for an intimate relationship with each one of us. She will challenge you to look deep into your own soul, then bravely lift your gaze to our Savior's eyes - and assures you that your gaze will be lovingly returned."

~ Amy Lively, The Neighborhood Café

"With honesty and vulnerability, accompanied with the power and truth of God's Word, Rivera Douthit nails true intimacy in the life of a Christ-follower. Clear understanding is given to those who have sought to comprehend the depth and importance of a raw, authentic relationship with Jesus Christ, as He so greatly desires, bringing rest, strength and healing to the human heart and soul. Whether you are a seasoned Christ follower, a new believer, or someone who is possibly just curious, this book will display the unlimited beauty and significance of true intimacy."

~ Cammie Wilson, Pastor of Women's Ministries

"Rivera Douthit was clearly filled with the Holy Spirit as she wrote her first book, *Intimacy*. If you are searching for a richer relationship with the Lover of your soul, I highly recommend this book!

~ Cheryl Pelton Lutz, Securely Held, LLC

"Rivera Douthit writes compelling personal accounts of intimacy with God inspiring you to settle for nothing less than a full elation of joy bellowing out from the deepest recesses of your soul."

~ Edy Sutherland, author of The WHEE Factor: The RUSH You Get When You Experience God in Everyday Life

Blessings,

Oneira

Eph. 3:20-21

Intimacy

into me You see

Intimacy

into me You see

Rivera Douthit

Hunley Press

Intimacy: into me You see

Copyright © 2014 by Rivera Douthit

Cover design: Rivera Douthit, Hunter Douthit, and Haley Douthit
Cover Photography: Rivera Douthit
Editor: Carole Ann Loebs
Contributing Editors: Carol McCall, Mary Anderson, Ranessa Thomas

Hunley Press
P.O. Box 473
Mt. Mourne, NC 28123

To my husband and best friend, David.
Thank you for loving me with agape.
You complete me. xoxo

Thank you...

Father, Jesus, and Holy Spirit for true and lasting intimacy. For loving, forgiving, and rescuing your girl. For guiding me on this journey. For writing when I didn't know what to write. For being faithful and true to your promises.

David for loving me through. Your heart amazes me. Words aren't enough.

Hunter and Haley for cheering and loving. You're my heart. (And where would I be without your computer tutorials?)

Mom and Dad for believing in me. Daddy, you taught me that ninety percent of doing anything is trying. Mom, you taught me courage with diplomacy. You both gave me the gift of an early introduction to the Love of my life, Jesus.

Keith for encouraging me to write. For marrying Jo and having Finley. She puts a smile on this auntie's face.

Aunt Cathy for reading and loving every word I've ever written.

Aunt Michele for showing me friendship (and make-up and fashion) as a young girl. Do you remember giving me that heart necklace? Some things I'll never forget.

Carole Ann Loebs for everything. I mean it.

Laurie Glascock for praying me through every. single. day of writing. Your friendship is a beautiful treasure. I see God in it constantly.

Tonda Huggins, one of my oldest and dearest friends, for praying and encouraging me through this process.

Cammie Wilson and Carol McCall for seeing potential in me, then cultivating and releasing me. Your friendship is invaluable and leadership inspiring.

Prayer warriors: Gennie Coe, Daniel Douthit, Audrey Malloy, Dean and Rachel Lentz, Evan and Donna Loebs, Ken and Jenny Wilkinson, Donna Bostick, Carol McCall, Elizabeth Loebs, Lisa Kelley, and so many others.

Marianne Campbell for believing in me enough to ask me to write for the devotion's team. You are a teacher and encourager.

Allison Herrin and Denise Blackwell for the generous gift of your time.

Mary Hempen for the generous cabin getaway where God began to stir in my spirit that it was finally time to write this book.

Jeanine Edmondson for opening your home. Janet and Jeanine for showing me that glorious Folly Beach sunset.

Cammie Wilson, Reiko Wright, Cynthia Ross, Lea Mikosz, Pamela Nogueira, Joanna Adkins, Elizabeth Galeski-Van Heck, Kay Woolledge, Cheryl Pelton Lutz, Mary Anderson, Jane Hassan, and Sheri Dimaggio for praying and encouraging. You each inspire me to be a better cheerleader!!

For the many others who have prayed and encouraged, thank you! (You know who you are!)

Some of you lived these stories with me. Some of you prayed to help me in the writing of them. I pray God blesses all of you a thousand times for all the ways you've blessed me through friendship, prayer, and encouragement. I stand amazed. Love...

Foreword

That undefinable thing we long for from birth to death-intimacy. Fortunately for you and me, there are writers like Rivera Douthit who dare to to share their personal testimonies of encountering Intimacy. The book you have in your hands tells of an intimate love story. One that is being written still to this day. As it addresses the real questions of love, grief, friendship, and marriage, it continually tunes our gaze higher--above our immediate fixations, above our longings for earthly intimacy into the most real place of companionship with our Maker.

In Intimacy, Rivera Douthit emphasizes this unknown, invisible, formula-free affection, and how to have it.

Through treasure-memories & stories wrapped in truth, she shares the hurtles, sacrifices, and victories of being willing to be known. Known by God. Known by people.

These revealing personal glimpses, combined with relevant biblical teaching, will lead you into a deeper place of freedom in intimacy.

This book gives honest direction in having true, healthy, and passionate intimacy in areas of:

- Friendships

- Grief

- Healing

- Marriage

- Loving God

I've had the inexplicable joy to walk through most of these encounters with Rivera. Get excited because what she has received, she is giving to you... An encounter with God that will catapult you into the intimacy you've always been searching for.

Rivera- What an honor that God has chosen us to be intimate friends. I am so proud of who He has made you to be. Ana Duo, me & you-o!

~ Carole Ann Loebs

Contents

Introduction

Intimacy /ˈin-tə-mə-sē/. It's not tangible. Webster's describes it as, "The state of being intimate: familiarity. Something of a personal or private nature." ˈIn-tə-mə-sē (into-me-you-see). It's allowing someone in to see us in the most personal way. Tangibly, I think of the difference in how we clean when our best friend is coming to visit versus how we clean when an acquaintance is coming. We allow our best friend to see more dirt. Real and lasting intimacy. I could tell you about it, but I prefer to show you. Come closer to see for yourself. Draw nearer and experience intimacy with the One who designed it.

If we haven't known intimacy with Him, we've barely touched on it at all. The intimacy we think we've known may have resembled the real thing, but authentic intimacy is birthed out of time spent with God. It's from that secret place with Him that all goodness flows. When the Lover of our souls is given His rightful place, the purest, most genuine intimacy begins stirring in other places in our lives. Marriages become stronger and more passionate. Friendships grow to greater levels of closeness and transparency. Our love and patience with our children deepens. Our leadership skills sharpen as we are led by God's voice and see others through His lens.

Now more than ever, the world is unpredictable. If there was an absolute place of rescue, security, and joy, would you want directions on how to get there? Throwing off religion and trading it in for a personal relationship with Jesus, there's rest in His presence. It's knowing and being known. We have it backwards, trying to achieve intimacy with God based on what we know about human relations. He wants our human affairs and exchanges to be modeled after ours with Him. He is the center, the Source, the wellspring of life to the full.

I'm convinced people long for more. They want a place of escape from the chaos of this world. They desire to be valued, noticed, and filled. God sees us and knows us better than we know ourselves. We search the world over for something to fill our emptiness and provide us with lasting intimacy. Jesus desires to give us everything we need and fill the deepest yearnings of our souls. He's the only One who can.

One

Into Me You See

"When the eyes of the soul looking out meet the eyes of God looking in, heaven has begun right here on this earth."

~ A. W. Tozer

The smell of old wooden pews, the sound of southern gospel singing, my grandpa's voice giving the final altar call, and seven years old mark the beginning of my journey with Jesus. I made my way forward and prayed the prayer. I trusted Jesus with all my heart. I always wanted to please the ones I loved, especially Him.

Years passed and pride swept in. Living by a list of rules, all the do's and don'ts, I had minimal tolerance for people who couldn't manage to walk the straight and narrow. In my eyes my clothes were starchy and bright white. Thinking I had it all together, I made all the socially and religiously acceptable decisions. Oblivious, my judgmental attitude was plain sin. I was a Pharisee. If I could've seen the truth, I would've seen the mud all over my starchy clothes.

Through my twenties I religiously attended church and served, often with wrong motives. Noticing discrepancies, it seemed *many Christians wore a costume and a smile on Sundays to disillusion others into thinking their lives were perfect!* The enemy slowly crept into my thoughts! A circumstance here, a thought there, a comment, a loss, a betrayal, one thing after another attempted to erode the truth and fabric of my thoughts.

By my early thirties, I had so much to be thankful for and couldn't see it through my exhausted, jaded vision. Our children were small and my husband and I were juggling our babies and jobs. We often passed each other in the night. Everything looked good on the outside, but inside was falling apart. Now *I had become the Christian wearing a costume and smiling on Sundays to disillusion others into thinking my life was perfect!*

The deceiver lied and manipulated his way in. I thought, "My husband's not the same person. He acts miserable. He must not love me. Church is filled with people masquerading as something they're not. Most serve to wave their badges and gain good standing with God, while others to minimize feelings of guilt. I've worked and been a good girl for years. Still, I don't feel any closer to God. As a matter of fact, I can't feel Him at all. I'm spiritually dried up and withering. Reading my Bible feels purposeless. God must not hear my prayers, because He's not answering them. What I've been taught my whole life must not be right; maybe it's not even real. Is God even real?" All logic and reason were depleted. Satan built his case. Thoughts were the first thing tangled in his carefully woven web. Actions followed. He set his trap and I fell in.

> *But each one is tempted when he is drawn away by his own desires and enticed. Then, when desire has conceived, it gives birth to sin; and sin, when it is full-grown, brings forth death. Do not be deceived, my beloved brethren (James 1:14-16).*

Apart from taste-testing a sip of wine here or there, I had never been a drinker. Most of my life people tried to get me to drink. Finally, I caved. Thoughts were tangled, desire conceived and *gave birth to sin.* Alcohol impaired my ability to reason or care, then temptation and sin followed! I never became addicted to liquor, but it was always a useful accomplice in my wrongdoing.

The following day always embraced memories of every careless action! In the beginning, I thought, "Now that I've done this, I guess if I died I could say I'd really lived." What deception! This went on for months. Fun quickly faded, and inside I was dying. My rebellious, confused heart was miserable.

Jesus had taken up residence in my life many years prior. He still loved me, but Holy Spirit couldn't possibly be okay with my rebellious decisions. They went against God's character. He detests sin and can have nothing to do with it. My choices were completely out of character for a Jesus girl, and in direct opposition to the nature of God living inside of me. I sensed something had to change or there would be negative consequences. Something was going to die, but I wasn't sure what. Parts of me had already died. Maybe it would be my marriage, someone close to me, or even my own death. I wasn't sure, but I knew it wasn't worth it. Without a doubt, I could not live like this. I knew I was a woman desperately in need of rescue.

Grace was looking at me, legs covered only by the moonlight shining through the window. Ashamed, I begged Him to look away. Emotionally stripped, naked and alone, regret plagued. Holy Spirit was wooing and convicting. He called me to come closer.

A transformation takes place when we realize God sees us. We can't have a personal encounter with Jesus and not be moved. Holy Spirit convicts, draws, and fills our emptiness. We are changed in His presence.

The crippled woman who encountered Jesus in the synagogue could relate to being changed forever in the presence of God!

Now He was teaching in one of the synagogues on the Sabbath. And behold, there was a woman who had a spirit of infirmity eighteen years, and was bent over and could in no way raise herself up. But when Jesus saw her, He called her to Him. (Luke 13:10-12a)

It was the Sabbath, a day set aside in the Old Testament for rest, and Jesus was teaching in the synagogue. Was she there out of routine or to get out of the house? Being physically crippled, isolation and loneliness were probably issues. Maybe she had heard of the miracles of Jesus and came to see and hear them for herself. Of course she wanted to be present. Perhaps she thought there would be some chance He would heal her. This woman had probably been shunned for, at least, eighteen years. No doubt, she felt invisible and unloved, but He noticed. We're not sure of her name, but Jesus saw her! Not only that, He was moved to action. He called her.

I imagine her looking around to make sure she was really the object of His attention. The journey across the room was risky. Considered ceremonially unclean, she would have to waddle painfully and slowly nearer, pressing through the crowd, risking ridicule and rejection. She faced her fears and moved toward Jesus. She had to! Her life depended on it.

My life depended on it too. I felt the eyes of the Almighty from His throne looking at me. Dare I come closer? How could a mess like me come closer to Holy? But that's what *Grace* does. He invites undeserving messes to come closer. Forgiveness, cleansing, and healing won't occur without it. The question is, will we? Can we? Or, are we too comfortable in our crippled state? But to live, we have to! The essence of our lives depend on trusting and coming nearer.

For eighteen years this woman had been bent over. She was hopelessly and helplessly crippled from a spirit, one Jesus indicated was from Satan. Of course every sickness isn't a spirit from Satan, but I've often pondered how the enemy gets to us, crippling us with wrong ideas and thoughts. Our minds and eyes trick us into thinking the way to truly see is by way of sin. The serpent taunted Eve with lies and used the lust of her eyes to trap her.

> *For God knows that in the day you eat of it your eyes will be opened, and you will be like God, knowing good and evil./ So when the woman saw that the tree was good for food, that it was pleasant to the eyes, and a tree desirable to make one wise, she took of its fruit and ate. She also gave to her husband with her, and he ate. Then the eyes of both of them were opened, and they knew that they were naked (Genesis 3:5-7a).*

I remembered how God had asked Adam and Eve as they hid in disgrace, *"Who told you that you were naked?" (Genesis 3:11a).* It was as if He asked, "Who did this to you? Who stole your innocence? You never noticed you were naked, until now. Who clothed you with shame?" Of course He knew, but He asked anyway. He wanted relationship with them. He loved them, so He wanted to hear their side of the story.

Why had I let Satan get to me? I guess Eve wondered that too. Aren't we all just a bunch of Eves who've tasted the bitter, blinding fruit of deception? As I considered accepting Jesus' invitation to draw nearer, the tempter screamed lies, "What's done is done. There's no turning back now. God will never forgive you. He will never use you." But, Truth told me different. He reminded me of love, and how Jesus died to cover every sin in the world, including mine. He had never left me. He reminded me of His promise--

Though your sins are like scarlet, they shall be white as snow (Isaiah 1:18).

On my knees, face down, I eased in closer. I cried and prayed. I came close enough to ask for forgiveness. He touched me like He did the crippled woman and began unraveling my mess. These words came back to me,

> *O Lord, You have searched me and known me/ You comprehend my path and my lying down, And are acquainted with all my ways/ Where can I go from Your Spirit? Or where can I flee from Your presence? (Psalm 139:1, 3, 7).*

God wooed me back. He wrapped His arms around me and whispered,

> *I have called you by your name, You are Mine. (Isaiah 43:1b).*

IS THAT YOU GOD?

We know we've been noticed by God when we hear His voice calling us. We sometimes hear God call us to do things that seem humanly impossible. Part of the process is trusting Him to do what we can't, believing He will provide where He guides. Writing this book has been one of those seemingly impossible requests from God for me. From now on when I hear people talk about writing a book being worse than delivering a baby, I will agree.

This process started several years ago. Praying, seeking, and asking for confirmation, the past year I waited on the Lord. He assured me I was already in the process of writing the book, so I trusted Him. I always said, "God, I don't want to write a book for the sake of writing. I only want to write if You make it clear to me it's what You want." In August of this year, He confirmed through people and the timing of their words, "Yes, it's time to write your book."

I prayed, "Lord if I've already been writing my book, what is it in my writing that you want me to share? What do you want the book to be about?" In the middle of the night He gave me the title and premise. I wrote it down. *Intimacy--into me You see.* The next day without knowing about my talk with God and His answer, my bestie shared a picture on social media with hashtags *#intimacy #intomeyousee.* I knew God was confirming the book and title.

Right away God told me to set a deadline. As I prayed for His timing, I was sure Holy Spirit told me to complete the writing by Christmas. I knew this would be pushing it, but I mapped it out. With diligence, stewarding my time well, and setting mini goals I figured I could do it.

Every imaginable obstacle and detour attempted to throw me off course. I had responsibilities to mother my children and be wife to my husband, which are my first callings. I had also committed to help teach a women's class on discipleship. After saying yes to God about writing, I had two surgeries in three months, two of my friends died within two weeks of one another, and people I hadn't heard from in years--and some I had--came out of nowhere wanting to meet with me. I had written two chapters and somehow lost the files, not once but twice (on two different computers). Every week seemed to come with a new set of distractions and obstacles.

Completely defeated, I called my husband at work and said, "I give up. I can't do it. I just can't do this! It's humanly impossible! I thought God wanted me to write this book by Christmas. I can't seem to get clarity or momentum. There's no way!" My husband was silenced. He didn't know what to say or think. I was normally the one helping him see the bright side. This time I was beyond discouraged.

That same day my friend, Carol McCall, and I were in the middle of a conversation when God gave her a word for me. She basically said, "Rise up. Arise." Then she read Isaiah 60:1-5 over me. God was saying "Get over yourself and do what I'm asking you to do." That night God took me to Nehemiah chapter 6. The enemies of Nehemiah had heard about the wall being rebuilt around Jerusalem. They sent letters to Nehemiah several times attempting to have him meet with them. They wanted to distract him from finishing his project. They wanted to destroy him and thwart the plans of the Lord. Nehemiah responded,

> *I am doing a great work, so that I cannot come down. Why should the work cease while I leave it and go down to you?*

The Lord spoke to me through this word, "Continue on doing what I've called you to do. Be diligent. Don't be distracted by people. Learn to say no and stay on course with what I've asked you to do." I read on,

> *So the wall was finished on the twenty-fifth day of Elul, in 52 days. And it happened when all our enemies heard of it, and all the nations around saw these things, that they were very disheartened in their own eyes; for they perceived that this work was done by our God (Nehemiah 6:15-16).*

Holy Spirit nudged, "Count the number of days till Christmas." When I counted, it was 52 days exactly! God was promising that we would finish this book! He would do it, and it would be a display of His glory for everyone watching and reading. I was right, it was humanly impossible. *But, "the things which are impossible with men are possible with God" (Luke 18:27).*

Be assured, the One who calls is faithful. It seems cliché, but where God guides He really does provide. What we can't accomplish on our own, He can through us. He is the *super* to our *natural*. We can only do what's natural for us. But God can do far beyond what we can imagine. To Him, supernatural *is* natural. When we are weak, He is strong.

Jesus not only called the woman with the crippling spirit of infirmity to come to Him, He called forth her healing.

> *...and said to her, "Woman, you are loosed from your infirmity."*

He spoke what wasn't as if it already was, by saying, *"Woman you are healed."* Had He seen her healed yet? No, but He was confident she would be. Though there was no physical change indicative of her healing up to this point, He spoke forth healing.

Too many times, we don't speak with faith until we've seen the results with our own eyes. Perhaps a lesson could be learned here to speak what isn't yet with faith that it will be. I'm not talking about expecting to get anything and everything we want, if we speak it. Sometimes we're not ready for what we want. God knows what's best, and His timing is perfect. I'm simply saying faith in our mountain-moving-God calls forth, believes, and thanks Him ahead of time, even when we can't see!

His words, "Woman you are healed," were life-giving. How often do we have the opportunity to speak life and encouragement over people, but fail to do so? My daughter, Haley, taught me this lesson a couple of years ago. A few days after Thanksgiving, she politely baked me humble pie. I received an email from Haley's teacher. It read,

"Rivera, I just wanted to tell you how touched I was that Haley brought me that purple shell from your beach trip. It was truly one of the most thoughtful things any student has ever done! I told everyone at the beginning of the year the story of how my grandmother and I used to search for purple shells and how I still look for them now. She is so sweet!"

I have to confess, I was a proud mama. But I literally knew nothing about Haley's little act of kindness, until after the fact. Haley shared that she didn't want to tell me, because she was afraid I wouldn't let her take it. She thought since it had a chipped place on it, I would discourage her from taking it, as if it wouldn't be good enough. Or she thought I might think it was a silly idea.

The sad thing is Haley was probably right. I felt terrible. I had instilled this fear in my child. My words had done this damage at some point in time. My perfectionist tendencies had convinced her to keep the giving of a little purple shell a secret from me.

I'm glad God taught me a lesson about the power of our words, and so happy Haley could receive the joy of watching her teacher's face light up. I've decided, no matter what I think of an idea, no matter how childish or silly I think it is, I will keep my mouth shut! Until I can think of something positive and encouraging to say, I won't say anything! I will always try to let God filter my mouth, and hopefully my thoughts will follow.

> *Death and life are in the power of the tongue, And those who love it will eat its fruit (Proverbs 18:21).*

The Word who became flesh and made His dwelling among us, knew the power of words. He was the Word. He chose them with precision.

"Woman you are healed." And she was!! *"And He laid His hands on her, and immediately she was made straight, and glorified God." (Luke 13:12-13)*

What Jesus had spoken came to pass *when He touched her.* His touch heals the vilest diseases--physical, emotional, and spiritual. He knew she had been sick and for how long. He knew He would heal her on that day, at that time, in front of those particular people. I don't know why God chooses complete healing for some, and others He doesn't. I know sickness and death are, in general, the results of living in a fallen, sin-saturated world. Either way, God's plans for us are perfect. He knows what He's doing. Even when we can't see the big picture, we can rest in that.

Of course, this bent over woman didn't come that day with an expectation of being healed. After eighteen years of dealing with it, she had grown accustomed to her sickness. Sometimes we get comfortable in our own misery. We settle in our minds that this is just the way it's going to be. Satan wants to prevent the greatness God has for us by crippling us with the idea that we're going to be stuck with our current situation forever. Jesus said,

> *The thief does not come except to steal, and to kill, and to destroy. I have come that they may have life, and that they may have it more abundantly (John 10:10).*

What Jesus offers is always sufficient in quantity and superior in quality, meaning it's full in every way. He is Life, we should expect no less. He wants our healing as much or more than we do. The question is, do we believe? When He ministered to people for healing, salvation, and deliverance, He frequently told them their faith had saved them or healed them. Then He encouraged them to go in peace. The miracle hinged on faith in Him. Most of us believe He can set us free from our infirmity, but we can't imagine that He will, or that He would want to. Don't be crippled by the spirit of unbelief. God can and will and wants to. Choose belief.

When the God-Who-Sees saw this woman in need, He beckoned her to come closer. Moved by His invitation to be near Him, she eased in. Healing was absolutely the result. It wasn't a maybe. There was no doubt in Jesus' mind He would heal her. His word and touch changed it all. She raised up. He lifted her right out of her life of sickness into a new life, and all she could do was praise.

I heard a pastor recently tell a story of a woman who praised God with such enthusiasm during the worship portion of the service, people were uncomfortable and actually complained. The pastor went on to explain that she had experienced horrific abuse in her childhood. She had finally been set free. Her praise was a full expression of her thankfulness to Jesus for healing her from the torment of her past. I imagine this crippled woman, now completely healed, praised God with her hands, feet, mouth and everything in her. She simply couldn't stop.

FREE

Funny how we can be involved in church and know for sure we're forgiven, but still be stifled by shame. Several months had passed since that night I got on my knees with God. My husband and I found a new church, and I was already involved with serving on the worship team.

Soon after I joined the team, God told me to take the female worship leaders on a retreat to promote unity among the group, so I did. Relationships were mended, confessions were made, tears were shed. God was busy doing everyday relationship miracles right before our eyes. It was inspiring to watch Him do what He said He wanted to do while we were there. To my surprise, His plans were for far more.

Forgiven but not free, I decided I would go to my grave with all I had done. It was between me, my husband, and God. Still the guilt was so heavy. I remember my friend, John Carter, from the band saying, "There's a sadness about you, and I just can't seem to put my finger on it." Little did he know, I was dying on the inside. God had forgiven me, but I couldn't forgive myself. Another scheme of the enemy. As long as I stayed weighted down, I couldn't experience the freedom to do all that God had planned.

The last night of our women's getaway, my new friend and I went to take out the trash. After she confessed a secret stronghold, the Holy Spirit nudged, "Share your story."

A battle raged in my thoughts, "She's so young, she'll never understand. What if she tells someone. She'll judge you. What she did is nothing in comparison. What if you can't trust her?"

Meanwhile Holy Spirit continued, "Tell her. Won't you trust Me?"

I sat in the dark on the steps. She sat with the street light shining on her. This moment was illustrative of our innermost souls. She had spoken hers into light while mine remained hidden in darkness. It was like the separation of dark from light when God created, "And God saw the light, that it was good; and God divided the light from the darkness" (Genesis 1:4). The two can't marry. It's either one or the other. And in the dark closet of my soul, my shame was hidden. The enemy wanted it to stay that way.

I chose to trust God, and had to act on it or suffocate in the heaviness of the moment. Tears flowed as words came. As I spoke, Jesus cleansed. Word by heavy, tearful word, I felt more free. God gave my sweet friend wisdom and grace. As she spoke truth, I saw Jesus. *Grace* was with us, and I heard Him saying, "Rivera, you are mine. I love you. I died for you. Nothing you have done, or will ever do, can change that! You have to let go and move forward. You are my girl... forgiven, blessed, and treasured. I have plans for you. Let Me heal and set you free." He reminded,

> *"I, even I, am He who blots out your transgressions for My own sake; and I will not remember your sins" (Isaiah 43:25).*

We took more than trash out that night. Our soul-trash was discarded, and Jesus began recycling. As those words penetrated my soul, it was as if the heaviness was lifted. I could breathe. Life was being breathed into me again. If God could forgive and forget, then I could forgive myself. I had never been that free. I had never felt so alive. In a moment, my sadness was replaced with joy.

He noticed me. He pulled me *out of the miry clay and set my feet on a rock (Psalm 40:2).* I was one of His lost sheep. I wandered off, and the Shepherd went out of His way to find and rescue me. He forgave. He saw me in my mess and loved me anyway. He saw me in my guilt and set me free. I had known Jesus loved me as a child. That's what I was told, and I believed it. Now I had experienced it. Never before had I known His love like this.

If God over all, the Creator of the heavens and earth, can forget our sin, why do we choose to carry it around? He wants to delete it for His own sake, not ours. The result for us is freedom that gives us room to breathe and heals our brokenness.

While praying for the Ephesians, Paul declared that power has been given to those who believe. It's the same power He (God) *exerted in Christ when He raised him from the dead.* The same power that raised Jesus from the dead lives inside of us. Jesus raises walking dead people to life, like me in my guilt. How better can we experience little resurrections in our hearts, minds, souls, and bodies than in the presence of the One called the Resurrection and the Life?

Inevitably, coming nearer God is life-producing. This is not at all to indicate if a person is not healed physically, they're not close to God. It is only to say, intimacy with God can't help but cause what's withering to blossom. He saw me overwhelmed by shame, whisked me away to a women's retreat and loosed me like He did that crippled woman. He satisfies our deepest longings. When we see Him seeing us, face to face with Jesus, we experience intimate relationship in its purest.

There's an innate desire in every human to be valued. We want to be loved, and somehow being noticed is part of it. We want to experience intimacy, the lasting kind. Yet, too often we look for it in the wrong places. Intimacy the world's way gives the impression it will satisfy, but each one of us has a void only Jesus can fill. God knows us through and through, every detail. He knows exactly what we need and when we need it.

My mom shared a story of a teacher who treated the children as if she hated them. All of her students were afraid of her. They were afraid to look the wrong way for fear of having their hands hit with a wooden paddle. Jesus is not waiting for us to make a mistake, so He can paddle our hands. He's loving us back. Into me You see. Into us He sees. He wants us. He loves us. He's all about relationship with us. He knows and delights to intervene on our behalf.

It's the kindness of God that leads us to repentance. It's His love for us that leads to freedom, and intimacy with Him heals. In His presence new life is breathed into our lungs, life like we've never known. Dead things start rising. Fully alive, we carry Him into every other earthly relationship. No matter where we've been or what we've done, we are never too far gone. We are all messes, but He faithfully unravels. Jesus calls us, "Come closer." Dancing daily with the Divine, we get to know Love Himself.

Questions

1. In Genesis 3:11 God wanted to hear Adam and Eve's side of the story. He found them hiding. He gives us the opportunity to admit our sin and be transparent with Him. What is holding you back from talking to God? Are you afraid to be honest with Him?

    Take a moment to talk to God. Tell Him about your struggles and areas of sin. Speak it out loud or write it in a journal. If you're unsure ask Holy Spirit to show you the areas in your life where you need forgiveness. Ask Him to forgive and help you turn away from it.

2. Have you noticed yourself agreeing with thoughts that question God's faithfulness? Now that you are realizing the source of those thoughts, what are you going to do to strengthen your faith that God is Who He says He is?

3. Do you struggle with guilt and/or shame? What is the source of these feelings? Write down everything that comes to your mind on a separate piece of paper.

4. Read and memorize Isaiah 1:18 and 43:25. What are the promises from these verses? What does it mean, *your sins will be white as snow?*

5. Take the paper you wrote on and throw it in the trash. As you throw it away, let the truth sink in: If you've confessed, been forgiven, and are no longer living in that sin, you are pure in God's eyes and He chooses to *"remember your sin no more."*

6. Read Romans 8:1. What does this verse say about you, if the Spirit of God is living in you?

For soaking, listen to:

Bethel Music & Jenn Johnson "Come To Me" *The Loft Sessions*

Two

Longing and Belonging

"But you are a chosen generation, a royal priesthood, a holy nation, His own special people, that you may proclaim the praises of Him who called you out of darkness into His marvelous light;"
~ *1 Peter 2:9*

Standing in the front lawn at Brawley Middle School, I stayed for several hours waiting for my turn to try out. I could see myself in that little red skirt with those pom-poms. A Brawley Braves cheerleader--this was the ultimate label, the greatest achievement! I had memorized my cheer and practiced all the right moves.

"BE. aggressive! BE. E. aggressive! B. E. A. G. G. R. E. S. S. I. V. E."

I was shy as a girl, but I pushed through my fears and tried out anyway! I felt like I had done well but when they announced who made the team, they skipped my name. I questioned, "I guess I didn't look the part? Something must've been wrong with me. Was I not pretty enough? Was I too big or too tall? Didn't I cheer loud enough?" I felt as though I had been STAMPED with "not enough."

Life is a constant search for identity. The world tries to tell us who we should be! The enemy of our souls wants to tell us who we are! We get stamped with labels our entire lives. In my early twenties, I was diagnosed with Crohn's. Chronic illness--STAMP

Married--STAMP

Professional nurse--STAMP

An ended friendship. Rejected--STAMP

Difficulty getting pregnant. Infertility--STAMP

Birthed two children. Mom--STAMP

Turned away from God. Guilty--STAMP

Do you ever wake up and think, *who am I?   What am I doing? How did I get here?   This wasn't the life I had planned for myself! I'm a stay-at-home mom, but I really wanted to have a career. I'm a career woman, and I really wanted to stay home with my children.*

We wrestle, don't we? What really matters is what God says about us, who He says we are! I rarely share that I have Crohn's disease. Years ago I was diagnosed, but I did not let that define me. Crohn's doesn't own me. I never want to be known as that married, retired nurse with two children who writes and has a chronic illness. I'd rather be known as a woman who exudes the joy and love of Jesus, identified by who I am in Him and not by the labels the world has tried to place on me. The truth that my Heavenly Father is the only One with the authority to label me washes those worldly stamp marks clean off. I'm stamped with Jesus, and I know who I am because I know Whose I am!

DADDY

When I heard his message, I knew my daddy wanted me to return his call. With that, I knew he was probably going to be upset. Sure enough, words flew recklessly rooted out of hurt. My daddy needed time with his girl. I needed time with him. It was so difficult to say I couldn't be there. Every girl needs special time with her daddy, and we hadn't had that in a while, just the two of us.

God had asked me to take the weekend to be alone with Him for writing. Saying "no for now" to do what God was asking me to do was a sacrifice, and more difficult than I imagined. My dad works hard, and his expectation is that we all prioritize being together at his beach house on certain holidays. After getting the blessing of my own children and husband to write for the weekend, I told God I needed my daddy's blessing.

After heated conversation and lots of emotion from the other end of the phone, he finally let me talk. "Daddy this was NOT an easy decision for me. I went back and forth in my mind and with God all week. I knew what I was supposed to do, but I was afraid I would disappoint you. Hurting you is the last thing I ever want to do, which is why I didn't call you sooner. I didn't want you to be mad or upset, so I just didn't confront it. This probably wasn't the best way to handle it, I'll admit. But I hoped if I avoided talking, this feeling of letting you down wouldn't come. I really feel terrible right now and want to just give in, but I can't. Sometimes following God takes sacrifice. I live my whole life taking care of everybody else. I'm not meaning any disrespect to you at all Daddy, but I can't live my life for people. I have to choose between people-pleasing and God-pleasing."

Sharing my heart, I assured him my decision to stay away had nothing to do with me not wanting to spend time with him or with family. I wasn't rejecting him. This was me hearing God's voice and following.

He said, "Honey, if God's telling you to do something, then you know you have to do it. I didn't understand everything. I didn't know the details. I'm not mad at you. I was just feeling hurt. You know you have my blessing. *(The exact words God knew I needed to hear.)* If I could have my way, I would have my girl with us this weekend, but I understand. If I was ever mad at you, I couldn't stay that way. *You're my heart,* you and your brother both. You are my kids, and I love you."

Immediately, I felt the Father's heart rush through his words. I thought, *my daddy would do anything for me. He would give me the world and move mountains to get to me. He would, no doubt, die for me if necessary. This is how my heavenly Daddy loves me, but even more perfectly. I am His, and nothing can change that!*

It's not always easy for a girl to confront her daddy, especially if there's love and respect between them. It's nerve-wracking not knowing how he'll respond, if he'll be hurt, or whether he'll give his blessing.

We may avoid talking to our heavenly Father for fear of disappointing, fear of His response, or maybe fear of rejection. But He assures us we can come to Him boldly and confidently any time. We often assume He already knows our thoughts and circumstances, so what's the point? But regardless of what He already knows, He wants to hear from us. Our *Daddy* created His babies for relationship with Him. He desires that we come to Him specifically, so we can see Him in the answers. It's through straightforward communication with Him that we get His blessing, and our faith grows as prayers are answered. He offers solutions. He IS the *Solution.* He rescues. He IS the *Rescue.* He shows us love, because He IS *Love.* We may make decisions that dishonor Him, but His love remains.

Talking to His children, He said,

> *For a mere moment I have forsaken you, But with great mercies I will gather you. With a little wrath I hid My face from you for a moment; But with everlasting kindness I will have mercy on you, Says the LORD, your Redeemer (Isaiah 54:7-8).*

Why did God hide his face and stay angry *only for a moment?* Because His nature is to forgive and love relentlessly. Like the words of my earthly daddy, God says, "Honey, you are my heart. I couldn't stay mad at you." Tears surface at that thought. I am His heart. So are you!

THIRST FOR LOVE

Natalie's daddy, a drug dealer, was put in prison when she was a baby. He was released in the past year, but the hurt and emptiness from his absence remains. Natalie, in her thirties, is desperately looking for something to fill the hole in her soul. She can't trust God. Her earthly father was untrustworthy, so she expects that her Heavenly Father will be too. She can't let Him get close, so she chooses to be agnostic. Oh she believes there may be a God or a higher power, but she doesn't know Him or particularly want to.

Natalie gives herself away in search of true love. On the first date, she commonly sleeps with anyone who will give her attention. The problem is she never finds the love she needs. Mistaking sex for intimacy, she keeps giving herself away. She's continually used and abused. The lie that this behavior will ultimately fill the void keeps robbing her, and she is left wanting. She has lived with her current boyfriend for almost a year (longer than any other), but He doesn't respect her. Natalie is broken. Aren't we all, in some way or another?

Remember the Samaritan woman in John 4? I like to call her Sam for short. She had many husbands. The man she was living with wasn't her husband. When she met Jesus at the well that day, He offered her living water that would fill her every desire. Her attempt to fill her emptiness with one man after another always came up dry. Her thirst for love was never quenched. But Jesus offered her spiritual water that would cause her to never thirst again. Living Water met Sam at her point of need. He saturated her thirsty soul with truth.

He is waiting for every Natalie and Sam to come to the well of their lives, where they're trying to avoid embarrassment and shame and fill the empty bucket of their souls. He is Father to the fatherless, and wants them to know *Love*, real love, no sexual strings attached. He promises to never leave or forsake, to never reject or abandon. He's faithful, dependable and true to His Word. He's calling. He's the *Filler* she so desperately longs for. *Love* Himself wants to satisfy every parched, dried up crevice of our souls.

BELONGING

When visiting my in-laws in California where my husband and I lived for almost ten years, they graciously allowed me to drive their 4-wheel drive truck. I'm accustomed to driving a small car. This truck and I had our share of conversations with me apologizing for anything I might do in the next week to harm it. Despite my hesitation, I accepted their graciousness. Running over a few curbs and taking up entirely too many parking spaces, I drove it with a grateful heart. The truck and I managed to stay out of too much trouble. Then sure enough on the last day of our stay, (did I mention it had four doors?) I was pulling through the gate into their back yard. Unaware one of my children had left one of the back doors open, I pulled forward. Yes, I dinged the door as the gate slammed it shut.

The next time I visited, would you believe they gave me keys to their truck? They not only trusted me with it, they washed it and filled it with gas! Here we were again, me and that truck. Before leaving, I prayed, "Lord, please protect and help me drive safely." I was headed out to visit some friends in the ICU where I had worked. When I showed up in soaking wet sandals and pant legs, I had to explain.

The driveway was narrow with a house and fence on each side. The only way out was to back out. Feeling so good about my ability to drive backward, I got the truck turned around and thought, "Yes! I have managed to maneuver this thing to get out! It's a miracle."

Then it happened. Before pulling into the road, I glanced up and saw water shooting up behind me. This seemed a little odd and more fierce than a typical yard sprinkler. As panic rushed to my toes, I parked the truck and ran around to investigate. This was not a small hose or a busted sprinkler head. No, this was way worse. This was a real problem. It looked like a geyser. I didn't feel or hear anything when I backed onto this thing, and now the yard was flooding!

I ran into the house yelling for my mother-in-law, "We've got trouble. You might want to come and look." Emphatically I said, "I think we may need a plumber." My father-in-law is one of the town's most famous plumbers, with TV commercials and all! My brother-in-law, Johnny, and my husband are both plumbers. My mother-in-law laughed. I really didn't think it was funny, but she seemed to think it was hilarious.

To my surprise, Johnny pulled in during the commotion. My first time seeing him in a year, he welcomed me with a hug then ran down the street to turn off the water main. After assessing the damage, smiling he quietly said, "I think I can fix it. Good to see you again."

Thankfully, there were no new dings on the truck, and my mother-in-law kept saying, "It's okay. It's really no big deal." Her soothing words were a bigger deal than the actual geyser in her front yard. In years past, my relationship with my mother-in-law had been less than perfect. She didn't want her firstborn marrying a girl from North Carolina. Only in the past couple of years have I felt that she actually loves me. Her words and grace toward me in that moment saturated my heart more than the water flooding her front yard. It healed so many things. She really wanted me to know it was okay.

I saw a glimpse of Jesus in her. Her words extended grace and love. They healed more than my momentary anxiety. I finally felt accepted. She made me feel like one of her own. No matter how many times we ding the truck or run into the water pipes of life, our Father gives grace. We are often filled with anxiety, worry and regret, but He says, "It's really going to be okay. I have everything you need."

> *"And my God shall supply all your need according to His riches in glory by Christ Jesus" (Philippians 4:19).*

His supply is as endless as that gushing water main. My in-laws continue giving, when I clearly shouldn't be trusted driving their trucks. (Though I did notice the orange traffic cones in their driveway when I last visited.) My Heavenly Daddy does the same. He not only gives me the keys and tells me to try again, but He cleans the truck and fills it with gas. He meets all of my needs, and then some. Going far beyond what I deserve, His love for me doesn't depend on my performance but on His grace.

ROYALTY

She wiped down the countertop. Organizing straws and napkins, she said, "I like your shirt. I wish I could wear something like that."

I smiled and asked, "Why can't you?"

She said, "That would be pushing it, especially here at work."

I was wearing a black, short-sleeve sweater. Honestly, there was nothing outstanding about this baggy, see-through sweater. I wore a black tank underneath, so it was modest enough. There was no reason why this sweet, middle-aged woman working at Chick-fil-A couldn't wear a sweater like mine to work.

I encouraged her, "You're wearing a nice shirt."

She said, "Well yours is just so cute and feminine."

I said, "Thank you." Knowing this was about more than the color of our outfits and to make a point about perspective, I responded, "Well the way I see it, the shirt you're wearing is quite feminine. Yours may be even more feminine than mine. It's pink with beadwork around the top. See?" I pointed to the top of her shirt. She smiled, but past the color pink in her shirt I saw disbelief in her eyes. I went on and said, "You are beautiful!"

She continued, "Well thank you, but I certainly wasn't fishing for that compliment."

Grinning, I piped back, "I know. That's why I gave it."

Hesitantly she said, "I think maybe I could use a large dose of self-confidence."

Leaning around to see her name tag, I asked with a smile, "What's your name? I'm going to pray for that specifically for you." Pointing to her tag, she told me her name and thanked me.

As we were finishing up our lunch, the friend I was with excused herself to the restroom. Meanwhile, I went to ask for drink refills. My new friend bee lined straight over to speak to me while I waited for our drinks. I was amazed when she asked, "Have you always been confident, or has it been a process for you?"

Wow Lord! This is crazy! Obviously You are opening this conversation up again. What would you have me say to her?

These words poured out, "If you want the honest truth, my confidence comes from my relationship with God. I'm confident about who I am, because there's no doubt in my mind Who I belong to!"

She said, "Well, I would consider myself a Christian. I read my Bible and pray."

With confidence I responded, "Wonderful! Then God wants you to really get it. He wants you to know you are His beyond your head. God wants it to transfer from your head to your heart! Then He wants it to sink down even further, past your heart, deep into your soul." I asked her, "Would you consider God the King above all earthly kings?" She nodded yes. I went on, "Ok then, if you are a daughter of the King of all kings, you are royalty! It's plain and simple, royalty walks with confidence. Let that sink in."

I could see her processing what God had just spoken to her through those words. "Thank you," she said smiling, as she turned and walked away.

The girl at the register turned around with a huge grin, as if to say, "Yes!"

We are daughters and sons, and co-heirs with Christ, meaning all that belongs to our Heavenly Father is accessible to us. We inherit a child's portion. We belong! Our Daddy owns *the cattle on a thousand hills.* All the nations of the world are His. The *earth is His footstool.* Because we belong to Him, we have access to all of it.

Stopping in to chat with my friend over a quick lunch. I was clueless that God had ordered up some southern, sweet tea and a side of confidence-building conversation with a sweet Chick-fil-A waitress. What a gift! How blessed we are to be called children of God, and what an honor to remind one of His girls of her worth!

See what great love the Father has lavished on us, that we should be called children of God! And that is what we are (1 John 3:1a).

Our Daddy has anything and everything we need. He's chosen and loves us in abundance, and for that alone we should stand tall with confidence.

WHO AM I?

Chosen. What does it mean?

My friend Cammie shared how when she was younger, she dreaded teams being picked at recess. She was always worried she'd be the last one picked. With Jesus, we don't have to worry about getting picked. He picks us every time. We are on His team, and He has great plans for all of us. *To* Him and *because of* Him, we are enough. We make the cut.

For whom He foreknew, He also predestined to be conformed to the image of His Son, that He might be the firstborn among many brethren. Moreover whom He predestined, these He also called; whom He called, these He also justified; and whom He justified, these He also glorified. He who did not spare his own Son, but gave him up for us all—how will he not also, along with him, graciously give us all things? (Romans 8:29-32).

The enemy may say, "YOU'RE REJECTED."

God says, "YOU'RE MINE! You have value."

"The LORD has appeared of old to me, saying: 'Yes, I have loved you with an everlasting love; Therefore with loving-kindness I have drawn you'" (Jeremiah 31:3).

God loves us. He has drawn us with loving-kindness. Amazing, isn't it? Rahab the prostitute was part of the lineage of Jesus and His great (many times over)-grandmother. Ruth was a foreigner and one of Jesus' grandmothers as well. Deborah, chosen to be one of Israel's judges, led the Israelite army into a winning battle with the Philistines. Hannah, after years of infertility, birthed one of Israel's most famous men of God, Samuel. He went on to anoint David as King and advised him for years in godliness. David went on to be one of Jesus' great-grandfathers. And Mary, we can't forget Mary. She was chosen as a young girl to face probable rejection while carrying and birthing God's one and only Son. They were chosen and changed history.

Each of them were known, predestined, and called. God knew beforehand who they would become, how they would act, the mistakes they would make, and how He would use them. Each had the confidence and faith to realize they were called and act on it!

I love the beginning of Paul's prayer for the Ephesians,

> *For this reason I bow my knees to the Father of our Lord Jesus Christ, from whom the whole family in heaven and earth is named (Ephesians 3:14 -15).*

Interceding for the Ephesians (and us), he reminds them of their identity. It's from the heavenly Father that we, the family of God or believers in Christ, have our name. We are identified with Him. We are His. Our emotions often try to convince us we couldn't possibly belong. In those moments, WE MUST cling to truth.

Wide awake at 3 a.m., I stirred. Our hotel suite at the conference was plenty roomy, but my sweet friend, Reiko, had been sick that week before and was fighting residual sickness. I hated to move or get up for fear of waking her.

That particular night over dinner, we had transparently shared our stories in detail. It was all fresh on my mind. The next day, I would be sharing my passion as it ties to my story. The voice in my head was loud and condemning. It said, "Your sin was different, bigger, and in a category of its own. God hasn't possibly forgiven you."

"That can't be right. I know that's not right." I reasoned. Unsettled, I asked God to calm me. Frozen in silence and darkness, I tried to *take my thoughts captive* and give them to Jesus. I wanted my Bible but it was in the other room.

The nagging continued, "Don't you remember the Bible says, 'Do you not know that the wicked will not inherit the kingdom of God?'" I knew Paul had written that verse with a list of detestable sins. But sin is sin. If it weren't for the blood of Jesus, we would all be separated from God because of sin. Period! But the enemy is not above twisting God's Word or elements of truth to try to deceive. I thought, *If only I could get to my Bible, I could look it up.*

The voice continued, "You won't inherit God's kingdom. Who do you think you are? What makes you think God would ever want to use you? What makes you think you are worthy to write, lead or stand in front of women?" The battle was fierce.

I knew God wanted me to remind people of the freedom and confidence that would spring up out of a relationship with Him. That nasty voice in my head wanted me to believe a lie about my identity. I needed God to help me stand. I wanted to get to those verses in my Bible. I was desperate for truth and at this point, I was weary. I knew this was serious. Restless I prayed.

The next morning I woke up heavy, anxious, and feeling condemned. I saw a text message from my dear friend, Carol McCall. Word for word it read,

> "Rivera, I woke up during the night with you on my heart. I felt like something was wrong. No discernment about what. I prayed. This morning I thought you might need reminders of who you are. You are chosen. You are precious. You are called. You are Abba's beloved daughter. You are holy. You are righteous. You are pure. Do not listen to lies about your identity. Remember the power and authority of the blood of our Savior. Take your thoughts captive. Philippians 4:8 Isaiah 26:3 Colossians 3:17"

Good tears flowed. I was overwhelmed again by Love. He heard my fighting prayer and came to my rescue. Seeing Him seeing us, we realize we're valued and pursued by the Creator of all things. I couldn't believe it. Abba Father loved me so intimately and personally, He woke up one of His prayer warriors to pray for me, then prompted her to tell me. God wanted me to know without doubt that I belong to Him. God's truth and love for me washed over. He identified me. My label? Chosen.

I found my Bible. I needed to see for myself.

> *Do you not know that the wicked will not inherit the kingdom of God? Do not be deceived: Neither the sexually immoral nor idolaters nor adulterers nor male prostitutes nor homosexual offenders nor thieves nor the greedy nor drunkards nor slanderers nor swindlers will inherit the kingdom of God (1Corinthians 6:9-10).*

Yes that's what it said, but this was the good part... the PROMISE!

> *And that is what some of you were. But you were washed, you were sanctified, you were justified in the name of the Lord Jesus Christ and by the Spirit of our God (1 Corinthians 6:11).*

There it was! Truth! Washed. Sanctified. Justified. A child of the King.

Who we are is not identified by past failures, a diagnosis, family name, career, children, husband, boyfriend, accomplishments, appearance, or possessions. These may explain why we act and think the way we do, but they don't define us. Our Father calls us *blessed, favored, chosen, treasured, pure, loved, forgiven, and fearfully and wonderfully made masterpieces.*

My bestie, Carole Ann Loebs,' grandpa passed away recently. A wonderfully lovable man, he was in love with his family. He welcomed all of his children's spouses (affectionately named "the outlaws") into the family as if they were his own children. Giving to say the least, he and his wife had eight children of their own then adopted three from Vietnam. As Carole's mom stood to speak at his celebration of life, she preceded her comments by explaining how her daddy was unable to show her love. She had never known a father's love, so her most fond memories were the times her father-in-law hugged her and whispered, "You're my favorite." As each "outlaw" stood to speak, the truth came out. He whispered, "You are my favorite" to all of them.

We all long to belong, but to experience true and lasting intimacy we must understand who we are and Whose we are. As God's children we don't achieve our identity, we receive it from our Father! I am His favorite and so are you! This one and that one! All of us. We're all His favorites, and nothing--no action or thought--can cause Him to love us any less, not a thing!

In Him also we have obtained an inheritance, being predestined according to the purpose of Him who works all things according to the counsel of His will (Ephesians 1:11).

Questions

1. What labels have been placed on you by the world? How have these labels affected your confidence or lack of confidence?

God is a delighter! He loves to tell us sweet things. Read: 1 Corinthians 6:11, Jeremiah 31:3, Psalm 5:12. Ask Holy Spirit what He thinks about you. Be still and listen. Write what He says, and take it in. It's true. If you're unsure if it's God's voice you're hearing, decide if it lines up with truth from His Word or character. God would never say anything that goes against His character.

2. Have you experienced rejection? How? What was the result? Insecurity? Fear? How did it change your relationships with God and others?

3. Read Psalm 139 and Isaiah 41:9-10. What is a lie you have believed about yourself? Can you go back to the place in time when you fell for that lie? Ask God to show you the truth.

4. Read Isaiah 41 out loud. Speak your name in place of every "you."

5. What is/was your relationship like with your earthly father? How has that relationship affected your view of God? What are your initial thoughts about God? What do you think His thoughts are about you?

6. Are you trying to avoid something when you back away from intimacy with our Heavenly Father? Are there fears that hinder you from entering into conversation or alone time with Him? Tell Him what you're thinking and how you're feeling toward Him.

7. As a daughter of the King of Kings, what is one thing you are going to lay down (pain or lie) and exchange for your true inheritance (Isaiah 61:3)?

Invite Him to grow your faith. Ask God for something you desire. Expect Him to answer in His own way and timing. Know He WILL answer. Write your prayer below or in journal. Follow up and write when you see or hear Him answer.

For Soaking, listen to:

Jonathan David Helser & Melissa Helser "Abba" *Endless Ocean*

Three

In Love

"To love is to be vulnerable." ~ C. S. Lewis

It had not yet peeked over the horizon, but the sun declared it's coming as brilliant hues of orange and pink were painted across the sky. One of the most beautiful sunrises our eyes had ever beheld, it felt as though we had literally walked into a picture.

Waves crashed. Birds chirped. Fish jumped. The scene was spectacular! And wouldn't you know, before the sun rose, my phone camera died? My phone takes great pictures, and I had charged it all night, or so I thought.

Carole was with me. Her love for photography is similar to mine, and we both have a creative eye. Before my phone quit, I had a chance to capture half a dozen pictures. I knew she would get some great shots, but it wasn't the same as being able to take my own.

Frustrated and speechless, I witnessed the prettiest sunrise in history with no camera. Stunned for a few minutes, I entertained the thought that God cared for Carole more intimately than He did me. Maybe He favored her over me. I felt a little jealous. As I went to find a quiet place on the beach to sit and watch the sunrise, I heard God say, "Have you considered that I might want to spend time with you without the distraction of your phone? Besides if you love Carole, be happy that she gets to enjoy this time with Me taking pictures. I give you breathtaking sunrises every morning of your life right out your back door!"

Humbled, I said, "Yes Lord. I do love her! You know I do. I am happy for her, and I'm really sorry for having those thoughts. Forgive me. It's ridiculous for me to think that You would love her any more than you love me. I know that's not true."

It's so easy to fall into the comparison trap, isn't it?

After Holy Spirit shifted my thoughts, I began to take it all in. The sun was rising. God had my undivided attention, and I began singing "How Great Thou Art," an old hymn my grandma Daisy sang during my childhood. It was as if all creation were singing with me, as a huge group of pelicans passed right over my head in the pink sky.

Awed by the beauty of the moment, I thanked God and praised Him for who He is. He said "Rivera, do you see the sand in the palm of your hand? You can't count it, can you? Look at the sand on the beach. Imagine counting every grain of sand it took to fill this beach. Now I want you to think of counting every grain of sand in the ocean floor and all its borders. You can't do it. Not even close. My love for you exceeds all of the grains of sand in the entire world. Fact is, you can't wrap your mind around just how much I love you. I love all of my children that much–more than your human, finite minds can comprehend–and you are ALL my favorites!"

Meanwhile, Carole captured a beautiful shot of me sitting in the sunrise talking to God. No picture I could've taken would have been worth missing that one! Lost in an intimate moment with God, I was completely enamored by how He loves us individually, yet equally! Between the soothing sounds of the ocean and that spectacular sunrise, I was wrapped in the arms of *Love*.

FULLY KNOWN

When we are intimately involved with *Love*, we need quality time and great conversation with Him. Most women love to delight and desire to be delighted in. It starts when we're little girls and carries over into dating and marriage as adults. We dress, talk, even walk to make a positive impression. For most women, honest and authentic communication is a must.

The two most important communication skills I learned as a nurse were open-ended questions and listening. Knowing how to ask the right questions leads the patient and family to talk. Asking open-ended questions opens the person up to sharing more than "yes" and "no" answers.

Equally as important as asking is developing the art of listening. I don't mean being quiet while the other person talks, I mean really listening. When we've listened, we can usually repeat back what's been spoken in detail. Normally quality listeners also know how to ask great questions.

The first time I met my husband, I was immediately attracted to his ability to communicate well. I had always been a bit of an old soul, a little on the serious side. He could make me laugh like no other, and still can. Beyond that, he valued me in the way he spoke to me.

He was from California. Our families had known one another for years, and we had been told we needed to meet. When he visited North Carolina, we finally met. He was handsome, with a dreamy deep voice and a Californian accent. This southern girl's interest was peaked to say the least. I invited him to ride with me to Boone, NC for the day. I thought our drive would give us a chance to get to know one another. Four hours round trip he interviewed me.

David Douthit's actions made it clear he wanted to understand me. In a world where we're told everything should be about us first, he wanted to know every detail about me. He was interested in what interested me. To divert attention away from myself, I would suggest that we talk about him. He insisted we would have plenty of time for that later. Clearly in pursuit, he valued me by listening and asking well. Every detail was important to him, and I was intrigued.

We began developing intimacy in conversation in our first couple of days of knowing one another. He had asked so many questions, he probably knew me in the first week better than many of my friends. We dated 3000 miles apart for over three years, and our strength from the beginning was solid and transparent communication.

God wants us to trust Him enough to talk. Listening for His voice, noticing Him in the day to day, and digging into His Word we get to know Him. He already knows the details of our lives but He wants to hear them from us.

When my son, Hunter, was born, I asked my mom what she wanted him to call her. Because she was in North Carolina and we were in California, without hesitation, she answered, "I don't care what He calls me, as long as it's often."

I imagine that's how God feels with us. We don't actually get to see Jesus with skin on, but He sent the Holy Spirit who lives inside of us. Holy Spirit is how we experience intimacy with God. When we don't know what or how to pray, Holy Spirit prays for us.

> *Likewise the Spirit also helps in our weaknesses. For we do not know what we should pray for as we ought, but the Spirit Himself makes intercession for us with groanings which cannot be uttered (Romans 8:26).*

Holy Spirit counsels and directs. God manifests Himself in us through the person of the Holy Spirit. He listens and speaks, and this is how we see God. And like my mom wanting to hear her grandson call her often, God doesn't need our prayers to be eloquent. He just wants them to be often.

Hagar's story was a little different from mine. Communication had not been a priority and her man had not delighted in her. She really didn't have a man as she was Abraham and Sarai's maidservant. She had conceived Abraham's baby before her mistress, Sarai, could conceive. Out of jealousy Sarai mistreated Hagar. Abused and alone, feeling unloved Hagar ran into the wilderness. When she encountered God by the spring, He saw her and asked all the right questions. He addressed her by name and occupation. He knew her.

> *Hagar, Sarai's maid, where are you coming from, and where are you going? (Genesis 16:8).*

Then He listened as she opened up. She explained that she was fleeing from the presence of her mistress who had dealt with her harshly. As they continued this conversation, Hagar identified Who had noticed and called out to her in her rejected, lonely state.

> *She called the name of the Lord who spoke to her, "You-Are-the-God-Who-Sees;" for she said, "Have I also here seen Him who sees me?" (Genesis 16:13).*

Hagar saw Him seeing her. Isn't this intimacy? To see Love seeing us? She poured her heart out to discover the One who saw her and knew her fully. He even knew and announced that she was with child. There in that private wilderness, God showed Hagar He cared by knowing, noticing, communicating, and listening.

Most of us can identify with the wilderness of rejection, loneliness, betrayal and hurt. *Love* sees. The One who encountered Hagar in her wilderness sees our wildernesses. In *Love,* we are fully known and understood.

POWER LOADED WORDS

As I pulled into the driveway facing my husband's office window, it greeted me. I considered that he might be buttering me up, and no doubt it probably worked. I thought it was sweet that he had taken time to draw big letters and color them red. His choice of wording was lovely. The sign may as well have been neon, and it read "Hi sexy girl."

I thought, "How sweet! He still sees the girl he met in her early twenties, not the one who has graduated to the forties club with a few wrinkles, sagging skin around her–aheem–eyes, and a few more 'stories' than she had back then." I marveled at how he still sees me as beautiful after all of these years! "*For out of the abundance of his heart his mouth had spoken,*" well, his pen had written. "Sexy" was his word choice. Some may think that's a little distasteful. I would argue after eighteen years of marriage, if he still thinks I'm sexy it's a good thing. I had obviously been on his heart and mind. No wonder this man is my very best friend!

There was a commercial of a daddy with his smaller children. When the mom walked into the room, one of the children asked, "Daddy, why is mommy so pretty?" The man in the commercial looked at his wife and smiled.

Before we had our children, my husband loved that commercial. He would hug me with a smile and say, "When we have children, that's what they are going to say about their mama!" Simple, sweet comments can make the biggest difference. They can bring a grown woman to good tears. They can cause her to want to do pretty much anything for her man, and think he's the best thing in the world. Like the words of the woman in Song of Solomon,

> *Like an apple tree among the trees of the forest is my lover among the young men. I delight to sit in his shade, and his fruit is sweet to my taste (2:3).*

Isn't it nice to be delighted in by our husbands? After all, that's what every girl wants. To know she's his one and only. To know when she's away from him, she's on his mind and that he still finds her sexy. When we're confident of our man's delight in us, we delight to *sit in his shade*. His *fruit is sweet to our taste*. Pretty much everything about him is sweet to us. He's the very best.

Though our husband's words hold great weight, it's not fair that we look to them for our security and confidence. Imperfect humans, our husbands will mess up, but God is perfect. He *is* love and His love for us is perfect. Our confidence, contentment and security should come from Him. When we find ourselves contented in God's love, *His fruit is sweet to our taste.* Like the Psalmist, we can say we've *tasted and seen that the Lord is good.*

Words are powerful, aren't they? If the words of the men in our lives have that much power to encourage and change our attitudes, how much more do God's words carry the weight to change us and move us toward love? God's Word is alive. He delights in us and has a Word for us every single day, if we'll take the time to listen.

Like my husband, God doesn't care how old I get or how imperfect I am. I'm still His girl. So are you. He delights to delight in us. He tells us if we *delight (ourselves) in the Him, He will give (us) the desires of our hearts (Psalm 37:4).* He'll show Himself if we ask. We'll begin to see Him all around–all in our business–and get to experience how it feels to have the God of the universe doting on us.

If God's words and the words of our men have the power to move us, how much power do our words have to move others including our children toward love? As moms, sisters, aunts, grandmas, teachers, coaches, we have the opportunity every day to encourage our children and the younger generation. God has placed them in our lives and given us the responsibility of being role models. It's important that we listen well to influence well. We need to know what's going on with them and what interests them. God's entrusted us with helping them discover their strengths and God-given gifts. We not only play with them, but we pray with them. We teach them how to pray, and how to hear from God. We teach them the importance of praying with belief.

Several years ago, we were headed to buy groceries. My son asked, "Mom, why is everything so brown? Is the grass dying? Won't the animals die?"

I thought, "Extremely observant for a little guy." I answered, "It's dry because there's been no rain. And yes honey, some of the animals and plants might die if there's no water."

Inquiring again, he went on, "Why wouldn't God make it rain then? Does He want the animals to die?"

Under my breath I prayed, "Lord, how would You have me answer this?" I really felt like God wanted me to use this as a teaching moment, but I wasn't sure how to proceed.

Holy Spirit nudged me, "Tell him to pray."

I questioned, "You want me to have him pray? For rain? We've had no rain for weeks. There's only a tiny cloud in the sky off in the distance! Seriously?"

He said, "Yes, encourage him to pray. He needs to learn to trust Me."

I was reminded of child-like faith,

> *Jesus said, "Let the little children come to me, and do not hinder them, for the kingdom of heaven belongs to such as these" (Matthew 19:14).*

I knew stepping out and spurring my son on to pray for rain in the middle of a drought had more to do with me trusting God than Hunter. I realized this was going to grow my faith while growing his, (and even Haley's as she listened to our conversation).

I answered, "No honey, I really don't think God wants the animals to die. But I do think He's waiting for someone to ask for rain. Have you ever thought maybe He hasn't given us rain because nobody's thought to ask Him for it?"

He replied, "Mom, do you think I should ask God to make it rain?"

I replied, "Well, the key to asking is believing. Do you believe? We have to pray with faith that God is real, knowing He's listening to us, and trusting that He will do what we're asking Him to do. So to answer your question, I do think you should pray for rain. Just make sure you pray it like you know it's already coming. And when you pray, tell God why you think we need it."

He said, "Okay mama." Without hesitating he prayed, " Jesus, all of our grass is dying and the animals might die too. Will you please make it rain so everything can live? Thank you. Amen"

Meanwhile, I pleaded quietly, "Lord, please show off today and cause it to rain. Do it so Hunter and Haley can see You. If You ever wanted to build our faith, please let it be now!"

We parked and went in to buy our groceries. Down one aisle and back, we were near the door when Hunter yelled with excitement, "Look mom, look!" The sky had grown dark and rain was pouring in less than ten minutes of Hunter's prayer.

Tears welled up in my eyes as Hunter ran back and forth with excitement. "He did it mom! God did it! Can I tell somebody mom, please?" God showed off alright! *With God ALL things are possible*, not just SOME things, ALL things. God IS real. God DOES see. He IS listening. He DOES care. He is ABLE! It's our responsibility to teach this to our children.

Our faith grew that day. Our hearts were saturated as a little of heaven rained down over me and my children. Rain poured to water the earth and I thought of God's words,

> *For as the rain comes down, and the snow from heaven, And do not return there, But water the earth, And make it bring forth and bud, That it may give seed to the sower And bread to the eater, So shall My word be that goes forth from My mouth; It shall not return to Me void, But it shall accomplish what I please, And it shall prosper in the thing for which I sent it (Isaiah 55:10-11).*

My husband was intentional about making that sign to show me how he felt toward me. God may not literally leave signs in office windows (or maybe He does), but He is intentional in His pursuit of us. Our words have weight, but God's words are even weightier. His words rain life by saturating the dry ground of our hearts, bringing it forth to bud. He hears a desperate mama's prayers, and He answers a little boy's prayers for rain.

NEW WARDROBE

Stumbling into the bathroom in the dark, as I sat down I realized I was sitting *in* the toilet not *on* it. Disgusting?--My thoughts exactly! I felt cold toilet water meet my bottom side. Admittedly, I had to fight with everything not to throw a complete toddler tantrum in the middle of the bedroom that night. I wanted to be mad and stay mad! In that moment, my emotions didn't resemble love. I actually wanted to strangle something or someone for leaving the toilet seat up.

Some think we fall in and out of love based on how we are feeling. Love isn't an emotion, it's a decision. It's a moment by moment choice to say yes, to move in closer. We choose to love unconditionally, even when we're frustrated in our marriages, with our children, or with the decisions of our family and friends.

It's *agape*, the Greek word for *unconditional love*. It's how Jesus loves us and one of the pieces in our new Designer wardrobe. I don't know of a girl on the planet who doesn't get excited about new clothes, especially if she's in love. Women enjoy dressing up, especially to impress their men. Every single day we have the opportunity to choose to wear the brand of *Love*. Agape is the all-purpose garment in our wardrobe that makes every outfit look good.

> *Therefore, as the elect of God, holy and beloved, put on tender mercies, kindness, humility, meekness, longsuffering;*

bearing with one another, and forgiving one another, if anyone has a complaint against another; even as Christ forgave you, so you also must do. But above all these things put on love, which is the bond of perfection. And let the peace of God rule in your hearts, to which also you were called in one body; and be thankful (Colossians 3:12-15).

This wardrobe consists of mercy, patience, meekness, humility, forgiveness, kindness. *Above ALL these put on love.* Much like the fruit of the Spirit mentioned in Galatians, our new wardrobe represents the presence of God in our lives. Love ties everything together beautifully, it's *the bond of perfection.* Have you ever noticed, we are even prettier when we wear love?

Wearing love is shifting our thinking. Loving requires taking hateful thoughts captive to say, "Lord, I give You my thoughts. I want you to adjust my thinking. Tell me what You think or how You want me to respond in this situation." Because I love my husband and want my love for him to resemble Jesus, I reason myself out of being permanently angry. I give my thoughts to Jesus and let Holy Spirit filter my thinking. Instead of wanting to hurt my husband for leaving the toilet seat up, I try to think things like, "It wasn't really all his fault. He was probably half asleep. I should've thought to feel for the seat before sitting."

Wearing love is laying down. I'm not referring to sex, though it is a vital and healthy aspect of love as God designed it between a husband and wife. Love is laying down pride, bitterness, envy, judgment, and any unhealthy spirit that would cause division in the relationship. The first and greatest commandment is to *love God with all our heart, mind, soul, and strength.* The second is to *love our neighbor as ourselves.* To love Jesus with everything we are and others as much as we love ourselves, we have to learn to deny ourselves. The quicker we learn it's not about us, that we're not at the center of the universe, the better. Laying down our propensity to always need to be right or have the last word, wanting what's best for the other person, and choosing to see the good in others is love. Refusing to count records of wrongs or bring up the past, love being able to say "I'm sorry" and "I forgive." It springs up out of humility.

Nine years had passed since we moved from California back to my home in North Carolina. Right after our move, it happened. The vile words flung at me and spoken over my life that night were spewing with accusations. Elements of truth were twisted with intentions of destroying. I later found out she had been speaking these words to others about me for months prior to actually speaking them to me. My heart was broken. We hadn't spoken since.

Needless to say, I wanted nothing more to do with her. Why would I ever entertain the thought of allowing this person anywhere near me? The accusations and words she had hurled at me were completely unacceptable! I thought, "No way! Never! I will never even allow myself to be in the same room with her. I have the choice and I choose not to be where she is at all costs."

For years we visited family, and I successfully avoided her. But over the past two or three years God had been nudging me to forgive. I would deal with it, pray, and feel like I had forgiven. Then at the most inopportune times a thought of her would surface. I would think of all of the terrible things I'd like to do and say to her. I knew this wasn't forgiveness.

My husband's grandma was having her 80th birthday. Her one request was to have all of her children and grandchildren together for the day. She wanted us all to go to church, then have lunch and spend the afternoon with her as a family. We honored her request. After traveling back to California to attend church with grandma, we were amazed as we listened to her play the opening songs. I looked up to see them coming in. I expected she and her family would be there. What I didn't expect was for them to sit right in front of us.

God has a sense of humor, doesn't He?

There I was with family watching, God whispering, and the discomfort of looking at the back of her head through the entire service. I was in the situation I had vowed for years I would forever avoid. I knew it wasn't coincidental. I knew God was forcing me to be in the same room with her.

God nudged and I squirmed. More difficult than looking at the back of her head or having to see her face during "seat and greet," was examining the filthiness of my own heart.

The preacher preached on the beatitudes, and to my surprise Holy Spirit used that preacher's words to begin changing *my* attitude. He went straight down the list. "Blessed are… Blessed are… Blessed are…"

> *Blessed are those who hunger and thirst for righteousness, for they shall be filled (Matthew 5:6).*

I prayed, "Yes Lord. I do hunger for more of You and to be more like You."

He whispered, "Then forgive."

As I sat on that old wooden pew, God prompted me to look inward. It was ugly. Inside, there was bitterness, pride and un-forgiveness. He reminded me how these were not from Him.

The preacher continued,

> *Blessed are the merciful, for they shall obtain mercy (Matthew 5:7).*

Holy Spirit whispered again, "Rivera where would you be if I had not had mercy on you? I'm a merciful, loving and forgiving God. If you want to be more like Me, you have to extend grace and mercy. You have to let this go and love."

"Okay Lord I hear You loud and clear, but now what? I can't do this alone. You have to do it for me. Please help. I'm the one who was wronged and now I'm the one *in* the wrong."

I turned the page in my Bible, and my eyes fell on these words,

> *But I say to you, love your enemies, bless those who curse you, do good to those who hate you, and pray for those who spitefully use you and persecute you, that you may be sons of your Father in heaven (Matthew 5:44).*

"I surrender, Lord. I really do."

The next thing I knew I was passing a note to her during the prayer that read,

> "I'll keep this simple. I choose to forgive you because Jesus does. I choose to love you because Jesus does. I'm surrendering to Him in this matter. Trusting you will come in time. I can't help but be cautious considering the words spoken by you concerning me. But I choose to give it all to God and *trust Him!*
>
> Moving forward, Rivera"

I realized I didn't need an apology. I didn't need her to love me back. But I did need to have my heart right with God. She may never change, but what was inside me changed and that was what really mattered.

Wearing love is what Jesus chose to do for us on the cross, and what He asks us to do for one another.

> *This is love: not that we loved God, but that he loved us and sent his Son as an atoning sacrifice for our sins. Dear friends, since God so loved us, we also ought to love one another. No one has ever seen God; but if we love one another, God lives in us and his love is made complete in us (1 John 4:9-12).*

We get to be Jesus' love to others. What a privilege! In a recent conversation with a friend, it was clear she did not approve of a family member's decisions. Knowing my friend had a story of her own--as we all do--I listened as she ranted about how she disagreed with this other couple's situation. I gently said, "You know none of us deserve the way Jesus loves us. Thankfully He chose to anyway. I don't claim to know who's right and wrong in this situation, but I do know Jesus tells us to love one another in the same way He's loved us."

If we have trouble wrapping our minds around how much He loves us, we can't possibly love others with His kind of love. Paul prayed *"that Christ may dwell in our hearts through faith; that we, being rooted and grounded in love, may be able to comprehend with all the saints what is the width and length and depth and height— to know the love of Christ which passes knowledge; that we may be filled with all the fullness of God." (Ephesians 3:17-19, emphasis mine).*

Most of us can't fathom that God became fully man to walk in the dirt with us, then died so we could live. Think of the thing most precious to you. Maybe it's your own life. For mamas it is most certainly their children. For men it's most likely their wives or children. God the Father loves His *one* Son as much or more than we love our children. Because of His love for *us*, He gave Him to die for our sins. If you've ever wondered whether you're loved by God, that's your answer.

Until we accept His love and experience it for ourselves, knowing it's *width and length and depth and height* is impossible. Paul said it *passes knowledge.* That means it has to get past our heads. Once it leaves our head and reaches our hearts, we've found it. It's with the heart that we find ourselves *in Love.*

> *Greater love has no one than this, than to lay down one's life for his friends" (John 15:13).*

Questions

1. Can you recall a time that you felt "fully known?" Fully known by God or by another human being. Why did you feel that way? Does the thought of being "fully known" scare you? Why or why not?

2. Have you ever looked for love in the wrong places? Take some time to ask God to show you if you are really trusting Him to meet your needs for love.

3. Read Proverbs 10:19 and 16:24. What does God say about our words?

4. Read Proverbs 31:26. What does it say about the woman in this verse?

5. Read James 1:5-6. What does this say about wisdom? What 2 things must we do to receive wisdom?

6. Now read James 1:26. What does it say about the tongue? What are some of the reasons people use their words to hurt others?

7. How have you been using your words? To build people up or tear them down?

Pray for wisdom. Ask Holy Spirit to filter your tongue, giving you wise thoughts before you speak. Invite Him to show you how your words can bring life to everyone around you.

8. Are you forgiven? Where would you be if God had not extended mercy and forgiveness toward you? Thank God in detail for how He's forgiven you. Thank Him for what He's brought you out of. Thank Him for how He uses your mess to bless others and glorify His name.

9. Is there someone in your life you haven't forgiven? Have you tried to forgive but continue to hold bitterness?

If what they did continually comes up, chances are, you haven't forgiven. When you can release them to Jesus and genuinely pray for and desire His blessing in their life, then you've forgiven.

Talk to God. Open your hands as you pray. Speak in detail the things that are leaving your hands--things you've held onto--and let them go. Give them to Jesus. Leaving your bitterness and assaults with Him will free you to forgive. Ask Him what He's placing in your hands in return.

For soaking, listen to:

Kari Jobe. "What Love Is This" *Where I Find You*

Four

Eyes Wide Shut

"The Holy Spirit stirs in us a joy and peace when we are fixated on Jesus, living by faith, and focused on the life to come."
~ Frances Chan

We were out of town on spring break vacation when my children said, "Look mom, half the lights are out on that sign." As I looked to see the sign I was mortified. Their eyes were fixed on a restaurant sign named after private body parts.

Sinking in my seat, I said, "Yep, they sure are!" The giggling that followed from the back seat let me know they actually read the sign and more than likely knew what it meant. My husband looked at me with wide eyes like, *is this really happening? Are they really old enough to know what that means?*

One of the biggest issues I have with raising my children isn't teaching them truth. It's not even living out the Word in front of them. It's protecting them. There are so many outside factors and influences. For years I've been singing them the children's song...*be careful little eyes what you see, be careful little feet where you go, be careful little ears what you hear, and hands what you do,* and so on. There's so much truth in that little song...*the Father up above is looking down in love, be careful little eyes what you see.* I'm not above reminding them of those lyrics to this day!

Our children are saturated at every turn with what the world says is normal. But what's ok in the world and what God says is okay are two different things. The fact that we as a society have reduced ourselves to selling food in association with vulgar names for private body parts is disgusting. And why anyone would actually want to eat there is beyond me. It's sad.

Sex sells. It's really disturbing that we can't walk through the mall without our children being exposed to soft porn. Victoria and many others have given away all of their secrets. Half naked men and women are plastered all over the malls. We have become so desensitized to darkness in our culture, most people see the billboards and brush it off thinking it's no big deal.

It's a slow fade to sin. It's birthed over time. We go through life with our physical eyes open but unable to really see. We become more aware of the darkness staring us in the face, attempting to corrupt our marriages and children, when we saturate ourselves with God's words.

> *Thy word is a lamp to my feet and a light to my path (Psalm 119:105).*

Knowing and living the Word is vital to being raised to life and raising up the next generation to walk in Truth. Jesus is the Word. Jesus is Life. Jesus is Truth. If we love Him we should love the Word.

We teach our children the Word by reading and memorizing, but mostly by living it. In the ins and outs of everyday life with your children, talk about God and what He says about various situations.

> *Therefore you shall lay up these words of mine in your heart and in your soul, and bind them as a sign on your hand, and they shall be as frontlets between your eyes. You shall teach them to your children, speaking of them when you sit in your*

house, when you walk by the way, when you lie down, and when you rise up. And you shall write them on the doorposts of your house and on your gates, that your days and the days of your children may be multiplied in the land of which the Lord swore to your fathers to give them, like the days of the heavens above the earth (Duet 11:18-21).

This doesn't have to be at night before bed or at a particular time of day, though routine is valuable. It just needs to be! Priority is important. What's meaningful to us will become important to our children. We demonstrate how we want them to live by doing it ourselves. They learn how to live by watching. They will do what we do, say what we say, and dress like we dress. If we want our daughters to dress modestly, we have to do the same. If we want our sons to show women respect, they need to see the man of the house being respectful.

Hunter, my oldest, sat in a special chair when I would cut his hair as a little boy. One evening while I was working at the hospital, my children (two and three years old) were home with their daddy. Christmas was in a couple of weeks, so all of my wrapping paper and scissors were out on the bed in the spare room upstairs. Hunter and Haley managed to climb the stairs without their daddy. They maneuvered the door open to the spare room. Hunter sat Haley in a little rocking chair. Apparently to him this chair seemed special enough. With the wrapping scissors he began cutting.

When I came in from work, my husband met me at the door with my daughter Haley. She was hiding her head under a blanket. When I uncovered her, I burst into tears. Every hair on her head had been chopped. Miraculously Hunter was meticulous enough to miss her ears and eyes. Her hair had just started growing and was cut in the cutest style. I could even pull it back with bows. He had cut it fairly evenly, leaving about a half inch. To even it out, I literally had to use clippers and buzz most of it. She looked pitiful. Weeks following, people in public would tell me how very sorry they were that she was sick. She looked like she had been through chemotherapy.

I never dreamed Hunter was paying close attention when I had cut his hair. From a very early age they absorb every move we make. We can tell them how to live, but they are going to do what they see us doing.

FIXING

We mamas should be proud and tuned in to what's going on in our children's lives, but it's easy to obsess allowing them to become central to our happiness. Really people can become more important than God without us realizing it. No person is capable of being everything we need. No person is perfect and holy. The only One we should ever be completely dependent on is Jesus.

I met with three new friends for coffee recently. During our time together, one was talking and spilled coffee on the table on her friend's phone. With the spilling of coffee came the spilling of tears. Her tears weren't just about a potentially ruined (expensive) phone. They were best friends and little did I know one was moving from North Carolina to Texas. I watched, listened and attempted to comfort my new friend with words, but as she sobbed I couldn't help but think back to my college days.

We were inseparable after meeting that day in music theory. So much in common, we went at the world united. We sang together. We studied together. We prayed together. This was a spiritually growing time for both of us. She knew all my secrets and I knew all her struggles. When I changed my major to nursing I also changed schools. But we made it. Our hearts stayed connected. At my wedding she was maid of honor and sang a song she had written, *Love Never Fails*.

This time the miles between us were longer. California was where my husband was from, so I went. At first days would pass, then weeks, then months between times that we would talk. I always thought there was just an understanding between us. We each had busy lives but our love for each other would never change.

My world came crashing down the day she called to tell me she had been engaged for a couple of months. I thought it was odd that she didn't call me right away. An engagement was too exciting to keep from one of your dearest friends. She went on to tell me her plans for the wedding but that she wasn't planning to invite me. She didn't want me to "have to spend the money." Not only was I not asked to be in her wedding, I wasn't invited.

I asked for explanations. Had I done or said something? No real reasons were given. She was moving forward in her life and didn't want me to be part of it. End of story. My so-called "best friend" decided to leave. She checked out of our friendship completely. I was left to wonder why. We didn't talk again for many years.

When friends leave, tears make their way. For months even years, I cried every time I thought of it. It was a desperately painful loss. I grieved as if someone had died. (Our friendship had for sure!) From then on Insecurity whispered lies, "It was all your fault. If you hadn't been so outspoken. See, you should never have been so transparent. You shouldn't share your heart. You shouldn't love so deeply, it only leads to hurt. You are incapable of having close friends."

Insecurity's friend Rejection said, "No one's ever going to love you again. Your friends are just going to get close, drain you, and leave. You can't trust people, especially women. If you don't let anyone get close, then it won't hurt when they decide to leave."

I fell for the lies. Some people choose to put up walls to protect themselves. For me the insecurity and fear of rejection caused me to try to control those closest, while keeping others at a safe distance.

I wanted my new closest friend all to myself. For fear of loss and abandonment I held on tight. So tight it was toxic, but I was oblivious. She had some areas of brokenness in her own life that lead her to depend on me. She looked to me for answers and happiness when she should've looked to God. Because I was so in need of someone staying and not leaving, the two created the perfect codependency storm. It was worship of someone other than God.

For years after I moved back to North Carolina, we tried to keep the relationship intact but we never could reach a healthy place. We agreed to go our separate ways. God protected my heart. Of course it hurt deeply. The feeling of loss always does. God knew I genuinely loved her, so He sweetly gave me a dream to show me clearly that she would be okay. I had peace after that. I knew she was in the best hands possible, His.

I learned the hard way, I'm not God. For this I'm thankful. I'm glad He's in control and I'm not. I have a fail proof way of messing things up on my own. Things go much better when He's given control. We don't ever need to play the God role in someone else's life or allow them the privilege of playing God in ours. We can't fix other people. God is the One in the business of fixing.

Fixing our eyes on earthly friends rather than Him for our happiness only leads to ruin. Our relationships, whether marriage or friendships, cannot withstand this weight. Eventually they will crumble under the expectation that they could possibly be everything we need.

Some of us think *we* are everything we need. We get our eyes fixed on ourselves instead of Jesus. We allow our dreams to get ahead of God's plans. We think we can handle our situations and function just fine without Him, or we get so self consumed we obsess over comparing ourselves to others. We don't want anyone to get ahead, be better, or have something we don't have. All of it can be summed up in one word, idolatry. Who are we idolizing? Our children, husbands, parents, grandparents, ourselves, or God?

Remember King Saul and his obsession with David? The people rejoiced after a great battle had been won. King Saul heard the women singing,

> *Saul has slain his thousands, And David his ten thousands (1 Samuel 18:7).*

David had done better than Saul in the battle. Word was getting out among the women. David was as famous as the king, if not more. The people loved David, and Saul hated it. Enraged with anger and jealousy, He set out to kill David. God removed His anointing and power from Saul. Saul's self preservation did not work out. God wants us to look out for the interests of others. He desires our confidence in Him to be so great, we can securely help others achieve what He's chosen and created them to do!

I'm convinced one of our greatest hindrances to greatness is our desire to be great! Are we building our kingdom or God's? Jesus taught the disciples to pray The Lord's Prayer, ending with, *"Thine is the kingdom, the power, and the glory forever. Amen."*

A couple of years ago as I was studying the Lord's Prayer verse by verse, I heard God ask, "Did you get that Rivera? Mine is the kingdom. It all belongs to Me, and I won't share My glory with anyone."

King Nebuchadnezzar didn't necessarily have difficulty with comparing himself to others. He just couldn't help thinking too highly of himself. His pride became His downfall. He prided himself in his accomplishments, not realizing everything he had belonged to God.

> *All this came upon King Nebuchadnezzar. At the end of the twelve months he was walking about the royal palace of Babylon. The king spoke, saying, "Is not this great Babylon, that I have built for a royal dwelling by my mighty power and for the honor of my majesty?"*
>
> *While the word was still in the king's mouth, a voice fell from heaven: "King Nebuchadnezzar, to you it is spoken: the kingdom has departed from you! And they shall drive you from men, and your dwelling shall be with the beasts of the field. They shall make you eat grass like oxen; and seven times shall pass over you, until you know that the Most High rules in the kingdom of men, and gives it to whomever He chooses."*
>
> *That very hour the word was fulfilled concerning Nebuchadnezzar; he was driven from men and ate grass like oxen; his body was wet with the dew of heaven till his hair had grown like eagles 'feathers and his nails like birds' claws (Daniel 4:28-33).*

God detests our self-absorbed pride. It separates us from Him. While fixing on ourselves it's impossible to experience closeness and intimacy with God. In the end, the only kingdom that will come is His. Everything else will fade. I don't know about you, but I never want God to have to reveal Himself as Lord by putting me in a place of isolation, insanity, and feathers growing out of my head. I'm good. All glory to God.

FIXED ON JESUS

Therefore, since we have so great a cloud of witnesses surrounding us, let us also lay aside every encumbrance and the sin which so easily entangles us, and let us run with endurance the race that is set before us, fixing our eyes on Jesus, the author and perfecter of faith, who for the joy set before Him endured the cross, despising the shame, and has sat down at the right hand of the throne of God (Hebrews 12:1-2).

Around age fourteen, a few friends and I ventured into the dark woods thinking it would be fun. Now I'm not so sure what was fun about it, but it seemed an innocent adventure at the time. In the black of night, we lost our sense of direction. *We wandered around with our eyes wide open, but we could see nothing.*

Tripping through vines and briars, we groped for things to hold onto to keep balanced. Snagging our clothes, we stumbled upon a barbed wire fence. Attempting to climb this dangerous, sharp-edged fence in the dark, we realized the seriousness of our situation. Completely lost, I began to pray. My comrades were not impressed, but I prayed anyway. I called on Jesus to rescue us. As we got ourselves over the fence, we looked up and out across the field. In the distance, directly in front of us was a tiny, bright light. Anxiety lifted as the light offered some hope that we would soon find our way back.

We think the darkness will be fun until we're so far out, we're lost. But Jesus sheds light to reveal truth and show us the way back home. Jesus said,

> *I am the light of the world. He who follows Me shall not walk in darkness, but have the light of life (John 8:12).*

The Light offers life to all who will draw near. Coming closer and following Him is having the hope and assurance of finding the way back to the joy, peace and the comforts of home. When we get our eyes off the Light, we begin to trip and grope in the darkness. No matter how far away we wander, Jesus lovingly guides us back, if we're willing to follow and stay fixed on Him.

Our eyes can be a source of great temptation, allowing the sin and darkness of this evil world to filter in, desensitizing us. Magazine stands and televisions are filled with nudity and inappropriate language that have become the standard and norm in our society. Movies for children are filled with adult themes and innuendoes. Darkness creeps in slowly but light will drive out the darkness.

Recently one of my dear friends confided, "I want nothing to do with my husband. I don't even want him to touch me, let alone have sex with me." She went on to confess that she finds herself thinking about a man she knows from her church. She said, "He works closely with me, and I often see him staring. In conversations he's thrown out subtle hints that he's not happy in his marriage." In her mind he's everything her husband is not. He pays special attention to her, which meets a need she feels has long been unmet. They've written one another and had brief interactions. Now she finds herself unable to shake these feelings. She knows it's wrong and carries a lot of guilt as a result.

Obviously there's a lot more to this story than a woman who doesn't want her husband. There is always "more to the story." That's how the enemy works. He doesn't typically destroy a person's life overnight. He slowly and subtly waits for the climactic moment when all falls into place, then he goes for the jugular, *"like a roaring, lion seeking whom he may devour" (1 Peter 5:8b).* There's an unseen spiritual war going on. So we must *"submit to God. Resist the devil and he will flee from us" (James. 4:7, emphasis added).* Satan knows prayer and the Truth from God's Word are our greatest weapons. Pray boldly then, and put on the full armor of God (Ephesians 6).

It's not the area most fulfilled in us that longs for more, it's those areas of brokenness. The empty places desire the filling. Who better to fill us than Jesus? When we get our eyes off of Jesus, we begin to succumb to temptation and sink in our own weakened system of values. In his essay "Equality," C. S. Lewis wrote,

> "The tempter always works on some real weakness in our own system of values: offers food to some need which we have starved" (Present Concerns).

Peter stepped out of the boat with eyes fixed on Jesus. The sound and the fury of the wind distracted him, and he was filled with worry, hesitation, and fear. Darkness crept up on him. His faith wavered and his eyes became focused on his lack of ability rather than on Jesus and His ability. His focus shifted to the world around Him and concern for his own needs. That's when he began to sink.

My friend was sinking in thoughts that what God had given her wasn't enough. She felt she needed more. She looked around to see what the world might offer and ironically found it at church. The boisterous winds of the world distracted. Her eyes became momentarily fixed on the darkness of desire rather than on the Light of truth. Just as Peter entertained the thought that he couldn't possibly walk on water, she entertained overpowering thoughts of what could be with this other man.

Thankfully, Jesus was there to pick Peter up out of the water and keep him from drowning, and He did the same for my friend. Her first step to being rescued was confessing and speaking her dark desires into the light. She told someone trustworthy who could speak truth over the situation and give wise, Godly counsel. Truth defeated the enemy's schemes in her thought life. By confessing, she fixed her eyes on Jesus. And the Light of the world picked her up and kept her from drowning. Today she couldn't be happier in her marriage, sexually and in every way!

SEEING HIM

Tonda and I were friends who could always pick right back up where we left off. The fact that she only knew *of* Jesus, but had no relationship with Him, hindered our closeness on some levels. We didn't always see eye to eye. Her idea of fun was a little different from mine and always had been. She was one of my childhood best friends, and I loved her regardless of our differences. I was rigid and probably a little too matter-of-fact at times about Jesus' love for her, but she loved me anyway.

Years later I shared my messes with her and how God had loved me back and healed me. I hoped she would finally see Him and surrender in the moment. As always she loved me no matter what I shared, but it never seemed to change anything in her. No story, no prayer, and no amount of love caused her to budge, or did it? Maybe God was using it all along. Things never look the way we expect or dream they will when God is in our midst. He was the only One capable of budging her stubborn heart, but for some silly reason, I felt like He needed my help.

She was coming into town for a birthday party at her sister's that weekend and called to let me know. She didn't always call me to tell me she would be in town. The fact that she did this time let me know she really wanted or needed to see me. Was it God who wanted us to see each other? Whichever, I knew we needed to get together. Her sister, Ginger, lived nearby so I stopped in the next day. The three of us spent the day together.

A few years prior I would periodically see Ginger in town and mention church. My invitations were to no avail. Outside of family, Tonda and Ginger were both painfully shy. Getting them to church would be a miracle, no different than the parting of the Red Sea, but I never gave up asking and mentioning.

Eventually Ginger and her husband came and never looked back. When Tonda visited that weekend, Ginger had been coming to the church I attended for a few years. She had experienced relationship with Jesus. Meanwhile Tonda was hearing God stories from her enthusiastic sister every week on the phone. She couldn't get away from Him. Over the course of Tonda's life Salvation pursued her. He constantly placed her in the paths of people who talked about His love and goodness.

It ended up being such a special Friday for Tonda and me, a reunion of sorts. I knew the party was the next day, and she was planning to leave on Sunday morning to head back home. I wanted to invite her to meet me at church, but God spoke to my heart, "Just wait." I figured she would be halfway home by the time church started anyway, so I waited.

Around two o' clock that Sunday afternoon, she called. I could hear her beaming. In her excitement, it sounded as though she were coming through the phone. "Hey baby!" she said in her typical style, just much louder than usual. "Guess what! I went to church in Ginger's living room this morning."

Surprised I said, "That's awesome. I thought you were going home this morning."

She went on, "I decided to stay, and I'm so glad I did Rivera. I heard your preacher on the live feed at Ginger's this morning. At the end, he asked everyone who wanted to know Jesus to stand. Girl I couldn't help myself. I stood up right there in Ginger's living room in front of my whole family."

I was speechless. I think I may have garbled something like, "I'm so happy Tonda." I couldn't get my mind around it. Words definitely couldn't describe it. It finally happened! I'd been praying for this for nearly twenty five years. Off and on I prayed, but I admit I hadn't held out much hope this day would come. But it did! Tonda met Jesus. She finally saw and embraced Him. He loved her right into His arms. She's never been better, and she and I have never been closer.

She's asked since, "Rivera why did it take me so long to give in? I wish I wouldn't have wasted all those years." But honestly it was all in His perfect timing and for His glory. God's the only One who could convict her heart and change it. John wrote about the sovereignty of God and how we have not become His children on our own, or in our own power.

> *But as many as received Him, to them He gave the right to become children of God, to those who believe in His name: who were born, not of blood, nor of the will of the flesh, nor of the will of man, but of God" (John1:12-13).*

He alone has the ability to lift the darkness of confusion and answer our questions, to give us faces reflecting Light. No messenger or message can change the heart, only Holy Spirit can. What a privilege it is to know and be known by the One called Light. He shows us His glory through His faithfulness. He makes a way in situations where there seems to be no way. To love someone we've never seen, we walk with and talk to Him by faith, not by sight. It's knowing without having to always see. Faith pries our spiritual eyes wide open to truth. With it we confidently say, "Your will be done God. We trust you."

> *Now faith is being sure of what we hope for and certain of what we do not see. This is what the ancients were commended for. By faith we understand that the universe was formed at God's command, so that what is seen was not made out of what was visible (Hebrews 11:1-3).*

Salvation is seeing and knowing Jesus intimately, welcoming His forgiveness and what He did on the cross. It's about entering into a love relationship with *Holy*. He honors a repentant heart that's purely seeking after Him.

> *Draw near to God and He will draw near to you. Cleanse your hands, you sinners; and purify your hearts, you double-minded (James 4:8).*

Holy Spirit counsels, giving wisdom to those who ask for it, opening eyes and revealing Himself in obvious ways. God gave us eyes to see. Unfortunately there are those who see the world clearly but are spiritually blinded. It's why Jesus turned to His disciples and said privately,

> *Blessed are the eyes which see the things you see; for I tell you that many prophets and kings have desired to see what you see, and have not seen it, and to hear what you hear, and have not heard it (Luke 10:23-24).*

We see Him when we hear the cry of a newborn baby, or a newborn soul. When a prayer of twenty plus years is finally answered our hearts cry *Holy, Holy, Holy!* God formed the world and all that's in it with the simplicity of a few words. Surely He can manage the affairs and details of our lives. By faith we live with eyes wide open and forever fixed on Him.

Questions

1. Read 2 Corinthians 4:18 & 5:7, and Hebrews 11:1. What do these verses have in common? Describe faith in your own words.

2. Can you remember a time when you became overwhelmed by your circumstances and got your focus off of God? What happened? What are some ways to stay intentionally fixed on Jesus?

3. What are your children seeing as they watch the way you live? Are you modeling how you're telling them to live?

4. John 12:35, 46; Romans 13:12 and Ephesians 5:8. Was there a time in your past when you kept something hidden that is now in the light? What were your fears about bringing it into the light? What was the result of shedding light on it?

5. Is there something in your life still hidden in darkness? Ask God for the courage to at least write it down. Pray for the conviction and desire to place what's hidden in darkness in the light by confessing it to God.

6. Read James 5:16. What happens when we confess to one another? Ask God for a trustworthy person who can hold you accountable. Pray about who you might confess to other than God.

7. Read 1 Corinthians 15: 58. Have you been praying for someone for so long that you have given up hope? Does this chapter encourage you to continue to pray? Write your heart's desire in a prayer for that individual now.

For soaking, listen to:

Bethel Music and Jenn Johnson. "God I Look To You," *Be Lifted High*

$\mathcal{F}ive$

Abide

*"In silence and in meditation on the eternal truths, I hear the
voice of God which excites our hearts to greater love."*
~ C. S. Lewis

She nudged her girlfriend as they rode up the escalator. He was headed down the other side. Pointing him out, she said, "See that man with brown hair? That's my husband."

Surprised, her friend said, "I had no idea! You never mentioned you were married."

She replied with a smile, "Oh yes we've been married for years. We've never lived together or consummated the marriage. Actually, I don't know a lot about Him. We never really talk but yes, we are married."

Of course this isn't a true story. As ridiculous as this scenario may seem, it's often the way we relate to Jesus. We claim Him. He's our Husband and we are His bride, but we don't spend time with Him. We hardly know Him personally. It's easy to become distracted with everyday routines and forget about Jesus, isn't it? But when something comes along and we actually need Him, then we remember. He wants us to allow Him into every aspect and detail of our lives. He wants us to communicate with Him all the time, without ceasing, in the ins and outs of our days. How else can we truly know someone anyway, than by quality time? According to Strong's Dictionary, the Greek word for abide means "to continue to be present; to be held and kept continually." In reference to time, it means "to last, endure, survive, or live." In reference to condition, it's "to remain as one or not to become different." Jesus said,

> *Abide in Me, and I in you. As the branch cannot bear fruit of itself, unless it abides in the vine, neither can you, unless you abide in Me. I am the vine, you are the branches. He who abides in Me, and I in him, bears much fruit; for without Me you can do nothing (John 15:4-5).*

This abiding implies perseverance, vigilance, and obedience. In this passage Jesus was giving His disciples a farewell sermon. He knew He would soon be going to the cross. When applied to us, Jesus is saying we are to continue or remain in Him. If we do He will keep and hold us continually, never letting go. In Him we will live and produce. We will bear fruit. This is a promise. The more we spend time with Him, the safer, livelier and more like Him we will become.

Have you ever noticed yourself acting like, even physically resembling in some ways, your friends? My closest friends and I use some of the same words and phrases. We laugh, dress, even talk alike. Two of my friends in particular, when we're together, people ask if we're sisters. They say we look alike but physically we are opposites. They see the Holy Spirit and don't realize that's what they are seeing. We are sisters in that we belong to the same family in Christ. Quality time spent with one another and with Jesus is visible. I can tell them just about anything and know it'll stay safe. I know no matter what they'll still love me. When I've

Abide

had a rough day, my friends help lift me out of my pit and spur me on to productivity and greatness.

If our earth bound friends and family can do this, how much more can Jesus? If we will *stay in* Him, we will have all of this and more. Apart from Him we can do nothing. Of course we can do things the hard way. We accomplish so much more and with greater ease when we abide, allowing Him to do what we can't.

While studying to speak to a large group of women, I felt I was getting nowhere. With scattered thoughts I prayed, "Lord, will you please show me what you want for these women? Please give clarity."

In my spirit I heard, "Go to your closet."

I questioned, "My closet? Do you mean my 'prayer closet,' or my actual closet?"

Holy Spirit said, "Go to your closet." Not sure of the reasoning, off to my actual closet I went. Moving shoes, dirty clothes hamper and all, I sat down in my closet with the lights off. In the silence, I decided to try to listen rather than chatter on in prayer. Listening can be difficult, but it is as important in prayer as verbally praying. Sure enough, in the quiet and dark of my closet, He whispered my message. I went in with no idea what to speak. I came out with the entire outline.

Does it always happen this way? No, of course not. The key is doing what Holy Spirit says to do, moment by moment. From that secret place with God all goodness flows. It's there that Holy Spirit speaks, counsels, and holds us. Hearing. Doing. Trusting. Abiding is being aware of His constant presence whether we're preparing to lead or teach, or whether we're folding laundry. When I heard Him I recognized Him, because I know Him.

Many people know *of* Jesus. Knowing *of* Him and knowing Him are different. The difference is abiding. People have difficulty being alone with God, because they have trouble believing. What we believe about God's character and whether we believe Him at all, determines how close we will get to Him. If there's an underlying question about His existence or ability to do what He says He can, reasonably we wouldn't be compelled to come closer.

I once made the statement, "Stepping out in faith is half the battle. God wants to bless us, but He requires us to trust and believe Him."

Afterward I was surprised by a man's response, "You have had a great life with great friends and family. God's not there for everyone. In fact, he never heard me when I did believe." These were my very thoughts a few years ago, and what the enemy used to entice me into thinking everything I'd ever been taught about God's existence and love were wrong. I responded to this gentleman's words by saying,

> "I hear the hurt in that comment. Just because God may not have answered you quickly or in the way you wanted, doesn't mean He didn't hear you. I have been blessed, you're correct. When life's been difficult,–and it has at times–I've chosen to believe in what I couldn't see. Trying to give thanks in the difficulty, I knew God had my best interest at heart. I knew He either wanted to work out something in me, or He was protecting me. We can't see what God can see. We don't know what's going on behind-the-scenes. I choose to cling to the verse that says, " *'For I know the plans I have for you,' declares the Lord,*

'plans to prosper you and not to harm you, plans to give you a hope and a future'" (Jeremiah 29:11). God loves you, even though you may not be able to see it. You obviously can't accept that right now, but I'm telling you He does.

Jesus would have hung on that cross, if you were the only person on the planet who needed Him. He would've done that for only you, if necessary. But salvation comes through faith. He is a gentleman and will not force us to believe. We all have a choice to make. I certainly can't change your heart, but I urge you to tell God how you're feeling. He has the power to reveal Himself to you. I don't. All I know is relationship with Him will rock your world in a good way. I believe He has plans for you that are far bigger than anything you can imagine, but you have to surrender and trust Him."

It really all comes down to faith, doesn't it? Jesus suggested we believe with child-like faith. Truthfully some of us think ourselves too intelligent for that! We need to have it all figured out before we believe. Some of us want to see God giving us what we ask for but don't want to commit to having relationship with Him.

But God has chosen the foolish things of the world to put to shame the wise, and God has chosen the weak things of the world to put to shame the things which are mighty (1 Corinthians 1:27).

If we could sum God up in words and unravel all His mysteries, then He wouldn't be God, would He? I've been asked why I choose Christianity over other religions. The answer is quite simple. Jesus is alive! The gods of other religions are dead. Jesus was raised to life, lives in my heart, and responds when I talk to Him.

Just as we depend on the word of a trustworthy friend to validate or persuade us, how much more should we depend on the God-breathed Word to give life and the sureness of salvation to our souls? Feelings, good works, intellect, or being a good person doesn't save us, Jesus does. The Truth saves. According to Andrew Murray,

> "People err because they seek something in themselves and in their feeling. No: the whole of salvation comes from God: the soul must not be occupied with itself or its work, but with God: he that forgets himself to hear what God says, and to rely upon His promise as something worthy of credit, has in this fact the fullest assurance of faith."

People challenge, yet God's Word stands. It is absolute, without error and final. If we believe God's Word is a myth, that changes everything doesn't it? If we don't believe God's Word is absolute truth, we can selectively choose the parts we want to believe. When His truth speaks against our way of thinking or living, we might conveniently find loopholes or ways around His direction. But God clearly says that we should neither take away nor add to His Word.

If the inerrancy of God's Word is in question, then there's a deeper issue. Do we really believe in Him at all? When we manipulate God or His Word to fit our thoughts or lifestyles, we make Him who we prefer Him to be rather than who He actually is. Then we've created our own God and become guilty of idolatry. A. W. Tozer wrote,

> "Much of our difficulty as seeking Christians stems from our unwillingness to take God as He is and adjust our lives

accordingly, we insist upon trying to modify Him to bring Him nearer to our own image."

If we believe that God is Who He says He is and that the Bible is God's Word-- as Jesus indicated when He said,

> *It is written, "Man shall not live by bread alone, but by every word that proceeds from the mouth of God" (Matthew 4:4),*

--then we must believe every word of it is truth. God does not make mistakes.

> *The word of God is living and powerful, and sharper than any double-edged sword, piercing even to the division of soul and spirit, and of joints and marrow, and is a discerner of the thoughts and intents of the heart. And there is no creature hidden from His sight, but all things are naked and open to the eyes of Him to whom we must give account (Hebrews 4:12-13).*

Fallible people misinterpret His Word every day, but He is infallible. If the Bible is in fact the Word He breathed and inspired, then it is as infallible or inerrant as He is! If flawed men wrote the Bible, does this mean it has error? No. Imperfect men were perfectly inspired by an infallible God. At some juncture, we must believe and trust that our perfect God inspired and carried His Word unblemished, through generations, using imperfect men and women! If He has the power to breathe it into the hearts of men, He has the power to have them pen it correctly and maintain it for all time without compromising its integrity.

Tozer also said,

"I think a new world will arise out of the religious mists when we approach our Bible with the idea that it is not only a book which was once spoken, but a book which is now speaking."

God is mysterious and we want to figure Him out, but Paul said it best,

> *To them God willed to make known what are the riches of the glory of this mystery among the Gentiles: which is Christ in you, the hope of glory (Colossians 1:27).*

The mystery is revealed through Christ. The mystery is Christ, *"Christ in you."* He is the One who mysteriously created in the beginning, then humbly walked this earth as a human so we could live. And through this Mystery we are given soul-life. Alive the Word speaks, and we are changed by His passionate pursuit and love for humanity. Do you believe?

> *So then faith comes by hearing, and hearing by the word of God (Romans 10:17).*

LISTENING

Listening to what He said to do, I went into my closet. It didn't make sense, but He knew what He was doing better than I did. People often ask me how I know I'm hearing from Him and not my own voice in my head. Honestly the more I spend time with Him the more I learn to recognize Him, like with a friend.

Once in a public restroom I heard a woman clear her throat. Right away, without previously knowing she was there, I said hello to my best friend. I knew she was in that bathroom without seeing her at all. We had spent so much time together, even the tone of her voice while clearing her throat was familiar. Don't underestimate the power of quality time with God in developing the ability to hear and know Him.

> *I love those who love me, And those who seek me diligently will find me (Proverbs 8:17).*

He's not going to deny us the ability to recognize Him if we're sincerely seeking. He knows our hearts and will reveal Himself in ways best suited for us and our personalities. Practically I use a few questions to determine if I'm actually hearing from God:

- Does this answer line up with truth from God's Word?

- Is this connected to what God's created me to do and who He's created me to be?

- If the answer is through the words of a person, does that person rely on God for wisdom?

- Does the nature of the answer line up with the character of God?

- Did the answer come in a way that is undeniably God--a way only He could've orchestrated--with timing, events, and people?

This isn't a be-all, end-all list, but it is a good guide for getting started. It's important to make sure your answer is from God. The enemy will use anything to get us away from God's will, including respectable things. The seemingly right thing can be the wrong thing if it's not God's thing.

Noble distractions can get us off God's course, so learn to say no and set healthy boundaries. For example, I was asked to work the childcare area at church when my children were small. I knew help was needed, but I knew my schedule did not permit me to add anything to it. I wasn't at all above working with children, but what I was currently doing was more in line with what I knew God had called and gifted me to do. When creating boundaries, it's important to stay focused on what's most important and what God is saying He wants from us.

Know your limits. My friend Laurie wanted to volunteer at the school where her children attended. When they asked her to drive the school bus, she quickly said, "No way." She knew driving a bus wasn't part of her gift set or how God had wired her. She is gifted in many things, but driving a huge vehicle with noise and distractions is not one of them.

Discerning God's voice is incredible once we discover how to do it. When we first realize we've been addressed by the Creator of the universe, the feeling is overwhelming. It's especially fun to journal, record, and remember ways we've seen and heard God. Being able to look back and read builds faith and sharpens our hearing skills. It marks our journey with Him by highlighting special times along the way.

If God gives you Holy Spirit inspired dreams or visions, write them down. If He shows you something specific and you're not sure what it means, jot it down. He may reveal it later. If you face a time when you feel like He's nowhere to be found--and you will--you can go back to your journal and remember all the answered prayers and ways He's demonstrated faithfulness in your life.

Being still and quiet in His presence is another way to tune your ears to hear Him. The psalmist encouraged us to *be still and know*

He is God (Psalm 46:10). When we learn to recognize God's voice in the stillness, we will know it during the chaos and difficulties.

For a summer evening in the South, it was nice out. Close to dusk, we set out on our bikes to enjoy an evening untainted by thunderstorms. We thought this would be a great way to get some exercise and have some mama/daughter quality time. Haley and I were riding on a little country, dead-end, low-traffic road near our house. For some reason I felt unsettled. God reminded me to pray for protection, so I did.

We were picking up speed downhill. Haley was in front, and we were going along smoothly until her front tire started jerking back and forth. The bike began fish-tailing. Suddenly Haley was tangled in her bike, being tossed down the asphalt road.

She landed near the side of the road, face up, screaming, "Mommy, please help me. Mommy!!! Please!! Help me Mommy!"

I couldn't get my bike to stop fast enough. This mama's heart nearly pounded out of her chest. I had no idea what I would find when I climbed back up the hill to my girl. With no cell phone, I was so thankful to see a woman running across her yard and down the hill toward us to help.

All of my years as a nurse hadn't prepared me for this. Helping injured people had never been a problem, but it felt different when my child was the one hurting. I wanted to puke. When I got to her, I could see right away that her right upper arm was broken. She was scraped with road rash from head to toe. Afraid she had other internal injuries, I let her talk but wouldn't let her move.

She was panicking, so I consoled, "Breathe Haley, but please don't move. You're going to be okay honey." I prayed, *"Lord, please let her be okay."* I rode with her to the hospital in an ambulance with her arm and neck in braces and pain meds being given.

After hours and a whole gamut of scans and x-rays, I sat in the Emergency Room watching her writhe in pain as they formed a splint to her broken arm. It started to sink in. Tears began to flow uncontrollably. I had held them in as long as I could. All I could think was, "She wasn't wearing her helmet. Why had I not insisted that she wear her helmet? What was I thinking? And why had I not grabbed my phone? I never go anywhere without my cell phone!"

I heard Him whisper, "She's okay. You didn't need those things. If you had had them, you would've felt like you controlled the situation. This way, you got to see Me. I intervened, didn't I? Her head has no injuries, My hand was her helmet. I sent a woman and her son with a cell phone to help. Were you stranded for a single minute?"

I prayed, "Thank you Lord! I hear You, and I'm so in awe of You! Thank You for protecting my baby girl." I couldn't stop praising Him!

He said, "Don't forget. She's My baby girl too. I love her. I have plans for her, and I'm going to use this in both of your lives."

Three days later, as we drove to her doctor's appointment, Haley said, "Mom, I think I know why this happened."

I asked, "Why?"

She continued, "God wants to see if you will trust Him."

I replied, "Honey, you might be right. I'm sure there are multiple reasons why God allowed this to happen."

She said, "You know mom, it's easy to trust God when things are going well, but it's harder when life gets difficult. "

I said, "Yes, Haley, you're right. Sometimes it's just plain difficult. And your mama chooses to believe that God is good. His plans for us are good, no matter how difficult things get. He will get us through it, and He'll probably teach us a few things in the process to make us better. I choose to stand on His promises: that *He'll never leave us or forsake us*, and that *His plans are to prosper us and not to harm us*. I know He's with us in this car right now, and He will work this all out for our good, somehow. I trust Him!"

This is huge. Each time we trust God, we increase our capacity for Him. We make more room for Him in the crevices of our souls. A life of victory isn't maintained by how much faith we have, but by God's faithfulness.

> *So why do you worry about clothing? Consider the lilies of the field, how they grow: they neither toil nor spin; and yet I say to you that even Solomon in all his glory was not arrayed like one of these. Now if God so clothes the grass of the field, which today is, and tomorrow is thrown into the oven, will He not much more clothe you, O you of little faith? (Matthew 6:28-30).*

Consider the lilies. They grow by abiding. We could certainly learn a valuable lesson from them, couldn't we? To know, that we know, that we know, with everything in us, that God is God. He is on His throne. He knows us and is going to take care of us. The lilies don't live forever, but while they do, they spend *all* of their time abiding. Not some of their time, all of it. They are magnificent displays of the glory of God as they open and reach up in a posture of worship. Even when the wind blows, they sway and rest in Him.

Recently my ability to *rest in* God in the moment was tested. He asked my best friend and me to step into an uncomfortable situation to teach us the sureness of His faithfulness. We were with a group doing street ministry. As the day passed, the two of us needed a bathroom break. After scanning the street for possibilities, Carole said, "Let's go see if the Barber Shop down the street is still open."

I thought, "The barber shop? Seriously?Couldn't we find a more female friendly place? I'm pretty sure they won't have a women's bathroom in a barber shop." Keeping my thoughts to myself I said, "Sure. They might have one. I guess it's worth a try."

The door was standing wide open. As I peered around the door frame, I saw a long, narrow room lined with men on each side. Some were reading the paper as they waited. Others were watching television. I noticed that every man in this place was African-American, not that color mattered at all to me. It just struck me as obvious. Equally noticeable, and strange to them no doubt, were the two white women standing at the door gazing in. After living in Northern California with all of its racial diversity, I guess I naively thought this was a thing of the past.

The gentleman cutting hair just inside the door spoke to us, as we stood unsure of how to proceed. With a huge grin he asked, "Can I help you ladies on this fine day?"

Carole smiled and said, "Why yes you can, if you happen to have bathroom we could use."

He declared, "Well sure. It's in the back on the right." He continued with a smile, "Help yourself. You can have anything you want. I'd *give* you ladies that bathroom, if I could!" Business was apparently good that day, and we made our way through the lineup of men waiting to get a haircut. To the back we went.

As I waited I noticed there were all ages: boys with their dads, middle-aged men, and grey-haired, older gentlemen. If I recall correctly, it was my first time in a barber shop and it was like something from a movie. In the stillness God said, "Get ready. You are going to bless these men."

I asked, "Lord did I hear you right? Bless them? How?"

He answered, "You're going to pray over them." True story. I couldn't make this up if I tried.

I argued, "Lord, You know I don't mind praying with people, but they are all men. I'm a woman. A southern, white one at that! What makes You think these men would want to hear anything I have to say? If You really want me to do that, please make it clear. I need to know I'm hearing You correctly. Will You open up a conversation or something?"

Later Carole shared that God was speaking a similar thing to her while she was in the bathroom. As we made our way back through the narrow room I spoke out with a big smile and said, "Well thank you for the use of your bathroom. Now you all know how it feels to rescue two damsels in distress."

They laughed. One of the barbers stopped cutting hair. Through the noise of the television he asked, "What are you doing here?"

Well it was obvious we had just used their restroom. I smiled and asked, "What do you mean?"

He continued, "Like, are you here to shop or just walk around? What are you ladies doing in town today?" That was it! God was opening the conversation.

I answered, "We are here with the group down the street bringing worship and blessing people in town with prayer."

Without missing a beat the barber by the door asked, "Well then, when are you gonna bless us?"

Grinning, I spoke up over the noise and said, "If you'll turn the TV down some, we'll be glad to." He turned it off. Silence fell. We had their undivided attention and they listened intently as we prayed.

My mouth moved and something came out like, "Lord, thank you for honoring us to pray over these men. I pray special blessings over every man and boy in this room. Allow business to grow and blossom. Leave them all standing in awe of You. Bless their families. Protect their marriages. Honor these men as providers and protectors of their families as they choose to honor You with their lives. Help them to be the Godly men You created them to be. I know You have special plans for each of them." Carole continued and prayed as God led. Then we ended, "...in Jesus' name, amen!"

With a big smile, the man at the door said, "I like that! I think y'all act like y'all have done that a time or two. Thank you! Y'all can come back and do that *every* week."

We thanked them again and made our way out the front door. I marveled how Holy Spirit gives us boldness when we need it and crosses racial, gender, and age barriers. We are the ones blessed when we see people through Jesus' lens of love. Abiding in Him in everything we do gives us the courage to be risk-takers for Him. We can always trust Him to get us through safely and successfully if He's the One leading.

THE DILEMMA

Admittedly a text from a friend recently fired me up. She asked, "Do you ever get in those moods when you wish you weren't a Christian, or when you wish you could do whatever you want without judgment from others?" It was a loaded question and she was serious!

I can't say that I ever "wish I was not a Christian." I know how miserable I was when I turned away from God. I was empty, anxious, depressed, and feeling lost. No way would I ever want to go back to that! Rebelling isn't what I thought it would be.

Being able to do "what we want to do when we want to do it" is entirely overrated. What *we* want is normally tied to some short-lived, selfish pleasure. We imagine it will satisfy but it doesn't. It's rooted in being born with a sin-nature. In Christ, remaining and abiding in Him, we are new creations. There's a constant battle between these two natures: sin's and God's. If anyone ever tries to say they don't sin, they are lying *and* sinning. It reminds me of Paul when he wrote,

> *I know that nothing good lives in me, that is, in my sinful nature. For I have the desire to do what is good, but I cannot carry it out. For what I do is not the good I want to do; no, the evil I do not want to do—this I keep on doing (Romans 7:18-19).*

So how do we overcome? Trust completely in the miracle-working power of Jesus. We overcome with prayer, by staying in Him and denying ourselves the desires of our flesh. Allow Him to be ruler of our lives. Ask Him to be Himself through us. In our own desires and efforts we can't, but He can! Jesus said,

> *I am the vine; you are the branches. If a man remains in me and I in him, he will bear much fruit; apart from me you can do nothing (John 15:5).*

I Am. He is. We are not. So when we are tempted to give up and give in to ourselves, that's the moment we choose surrender. That's when we say no to idolizing ourselves and what we want, and we worship God by trusting Him to deliver us.

Abide. Meet with Him in secret. In the quiet get to know the Spirit of the Living God. Listen and let Him lead. Trust. Apart from Him we can do nothing.

Questions

1. Has a hurt taken you to a crisis of faith where you are close to believing that God is not who He says He is? Have you poured your heart out transparently to God regarding this matter and listened for Him to speak to you? If so, what were the results? If not, are you ready to tell Him now?

2. Do you have trouble believing God's Word is absolute truth? Why or why not.

3. Read: 2 Chronicles 7:14, Jeremiah 29:13, Matthew 6:33, James 4:8. What does God encourage us to do? In 2 Chronicles 7:14, what is the result of seeking God in humility, prayer, and repentance?

4. Abiding is like plugging a lifeless cell phone into an electrical outlet for a recharge. Get alone each day in your recharging station with God. Let Him give what you need for the day.

Do you have a routine time and place to get alone with God? What are some hindrances to routine quiet time? What does it look like to abide?

5. Read 1 Thessalonians 5:17. What does this verse mean to you?

6. Read John 15:1-5. Who is the Husbandman, Vine keeper, or Gardener (depending on the version you use)? Why does Jesus refer to Himself as the Vine? Have you ever gotten ahead of God or tried to do something on your own? What was the result?

7. Read John 15:7. What does it say about abiding?

Begin inviting God into your decisions, big and small. Trust Him. He cares about every detail of your life. He wants to hear from you.

For soaking, listen to:

 Bethel Music & Jenn Johnson "I Love Your Presence" *Here Is Love*

$\mathcal{S}ix$

Hearts Wide Open

*"I will give you a new heart and put a new spirit within you; I will
take the heart of stone out of your flesh and give you a heart of
flesh." ~ God (Ezekiel 36:26)*

He was resuscitated three times in 24 hours. I had never been on
the family's side of it. Because it was Daddy, it felt different. The
relief was overwhelming each time the nurse reported him being
alive and stable. The other family in the waiting room helped time
pass. The woman's husband was having bypass surgery too. They
saw the fear in our eyes with each alarm and the voice overhead
repeating "Code Blue to CCU." Silence would fall, and I would run
to the locked doors of the unit as if standing by the doors was going to
change the situation.

Exchanging wonderful conversation about God in the waiting room,
our new friends (a woman and her daughter) shared stories of church.
It was fascinating to listen, as their services sounded a bit more charismatic
than I had ever experienced. The daughter in her thirties or forties had
lived through a near-death-experience. She told how she had prayed
during her lowest point and pleaded with God. She said, "I just told
Him He had not given me my children for somebody else to raise. I
just simply could not die because they needed their mama." I was
intrigued by her boldness with God. I had prayed for years, but I'm

not sure I had ever prayed with that kind of fearlessness. Emphatic, she said, "After that God healed me, and I'm a miracle sitting here today."

A couple of days passed and my daddy was sent to the step-down unit. The first few hours in this unit were ok, but I noticed there had not been a nurse check on him as often as I felt they should. Trying not to come across as bossy, which I've been known to do, I didn't say anything. Evening visiting hours were ending and my dad didn't look good to me. I couldn't help but switch to nurse mode. I noticed trends with his vital signs that raised concern. I decided I would stay around for a while after visiting hours, at least until I was asked to leave. I stepped into the hall, so my mom could tell my dad goodnight and head home for much needed rest.

She burst into the hallway with a look of terror on her face. She yelled, "Something's wrong with your daddy." I ran into his room to find him turning blue and unresponsive. What happened after that is blurry. I hit the call light and ran to the nurses' station to tell them they needed to get to my dad's room with the crash cart. They looked at me like I was crazy, so I ran to the Critical Care Unit he had been moved from earlier. I saw the red-headed angel of mercy who had been caring for him through his previous Code Blue occurrences. I told her my dad was going to die if someone didn't get to that other unit and help those nurses. She hurried over with her crash cart.

We stood in the hallway traumatized while they worked to resuscitate him--again. The family from the waiting room was leaving since visiting hours were ending. Passing us in the hall, they saw my mom crying and asked if everything was ok. When I told them what was happening, they asked if they could pray with us.

Words began pouring out of their mouths that seemed to lift the roof off the place, not with volume but with authority in the name of Jesus. They prayed and claimed the healing hand of God over my daddy's heart. Within seconds of that prayer, (one like I had never heard in all my life up to that point) the nurses came into the hallway. One of them said, "You can go in and see your daddy now. He's sitting up in the bed smiling." He was alive and my heart sprang to life! There's life in the name and blood of Jesus. Lives are saved when prayers are prayed in faith for others. In Paul's prayer to the Ephesians, he said,

> *Therefore I also, after I heard of your faith in the Lord Jesus and your love for all the saints, do not cease to give thanks for you, making mention of you in my prayers (Ephesians 1:15-16).*

A couple of years ago, I visited the Billy Graham Library. Fascinated by the vast multitudes he reached for Jesus, something stood out to me while I was there. He had a huge team of people working with Him behind the scenes. His ministry teams constantly sent leaders to disciple and raise up other leaders world-wide. This ensured that their message wasn't just about making converts, but it was also about making disciples. With each crusade, homes and churches everywhere had groups designated to pray. Many people interceded behind the scenes, praying thousands into the presence of the Lord for salvation. The faithful prayers *of* the saints *for* the saints is powerful!

Relieved, I left that night with new perspective. I had seen with my own eyes praying power. Inspired to pray for others, I was forever changed by that prayer and the authority we have with the Holy Spirit in the Name of Jesus. I had seen God's hand of protection in my life numerous times, but I had never seen healing like that as a direct and immediate result of prayer. God used those women to teach me a new thing, to pray boldly and specifically, to praise Jesus and claim victory in His name.

Paul continued,

> ...that the God of our Lord Jesus Christ, the Father of glory, may give to you the spirit of wisdom and revelation in the knowledge of Him, the eyes of your understanding (heart) being enlightened (opened); that you may know what is the hope of His calling, what are the riches of the glory of His inheritance in the saints (Ephesians 1:17-18, emphasis mine).

When applied to us He basically prayed our hearts would be open to see and know the hope of God's calling in our lives. That we would know our identity and inheritance as children of God.

Daddy's murmur had been identified. The valve was poor enough to warrant doing the surgery. In the gamut of pre-surgical tests, they also found a coronary artery blockage. He needed a valve replacement *and* bypass surgery. He was tired, and now it was time.

Most non-medical people like to call bypass surgery, "open heart surgery." With bypass surgery it isn't necessary to open the heart. It is bypassing a coronary artery on the *outside* of the heart with a new artery, so blood can flow freely to the heart. Valve surgery, on the other hand, is literally *open heart surgery*. The heart is cut open to remove the old valve and replace it with a new one.

It's tiring when there are hidden parts in us that need healing. God is the best Heart Surgeon. He knows how to see and remove anything that doesn't belong. He can even repair what's been broken. Bypass surgery is not His specialty. He prefers not to bypass anything, but rather opens the heart to dig in deep and remove every problem area. Like my daddy, we have to become weary enough with our sickness of heart to be willing to let the *Surgeon* do surgery.

> *Cast away from you all the transgressions which you have committed, and get yourselves a new heart and a new spirit. "For why should you die, O house of Israel? For I have no pleasure in the death of one who dies," says the Lord God. "Therefore turn and live!" (Ezekiel 18:31-32)*

Here, God was speaking to His children through Ezekiel. He wanted them to repent of their sin. Repentance is a type of heart surgery, and God invites us to actively participate. To repent is to realize there's sin, confess, ask for forgiveness, and turn away from it. Ezekiel told them to *turn and live*. The Hebrew word for *turn* is *shuwb*, the same word for repentance (Strong's #H7725). Notice, living hinges on repentance. Life is the result of turning away from sin. It's the result of getting sick enough to ask God to dig in and reveal what needs to be removed then allowing His help to remove it.

If the heart dies, the entire body dies. Spiritually, if our hearts are dead, everything else in us dies. Our souls have trouble breathing. We have no joy, peace, or confidence.

Paul continued his prayer,

> *...and what is the exceeding greatness of His power toward us who believe, according to the working of His mighty power which He*

worked in Christ when He raised Him from the dead and seated Him at His right hand in the heavenly places, (Ephesians 1:20).

Sleeping on the couch in the waiting room, the surgery had gone well, and daddy was in the Critical Care Unit recovering. Everything from families sleeping in waiting rooms to Code Blue procedures were familiar to me. As the first Code Blue after his surgery was called to the CCU in the middle of the night, my heart sank. Deep down, I knew it was my daddy.

IV bags hanging and monitors beeping, we attempt to resurrect dying physical bodies to life. We grapple for every breath and heartbeat. When death is inevitable, we grasp for peace in the midst. The reality is, we have no control over either death or life. God decides. Life is brief and fragile and our days are numbered. Paul was referring to death when he said he was *"confident, well pleased rather to be absent from the body and be present with the Lord"* (2 Corinthians 5:8). In other words He knew when his body passed, his soul would be with God.

I always wondered if my patients had the same confidence as Paul. If their bodies were to give way, would their souls be prepared to meet God? My heart cringed at the thought that maybe they weren't ready. When someone is dead, there's usually no coming back. Death simply can't respond, except in the case of the supernatural intervention of God. He is the only One with the power to cause a dead man to respond. That's what Paul was referring to in this passage in Ephesians. God has the power to raise to life--physically, emotionally, and spiritually.

Was this how Mary and Martha felt? I wonder. They knew Jesus was the Resurrection and the Life but they hadn't experienced it yet.

He allowed Lazarus to die so they might have a fresh encounter with Him. He wanted them to see and be changed forever.

The same resurrection and healing power that raised Lazarus from the dead and the same One who later raised Jesus from the grave, raised my daddy. That night I had seen the effectiveness of a prayer prayed with this confidence. I witnessed it and overwhelmed I said, "I want that. I want to pray like those ladies." I had seen the Resurrection and the Life with my own eyes. My eyes and prayers were forever changed.

In regard to prayers, James said,

> *And the prayer of faith will save the sick, and the Lord will raise him up. And if he has committed sins, he will be forgiven. Confess your trespasses to one another, and pray for one another, that you may be healed. The effective, fervent prayer of a righteous man avails much (James 5:15-16).*

There it is again. A prayer of faith will *save,* and the Lord will *raise.* Prayers move the heart of God. Then comes confession, not just to God but to one another. I've heard people say there's nothing in the Bible about having an accountability partner. I would argue right there it is. *Confess to one another.* Find someone trustworthy. Confessing as God leads is safest, of course.

Remember the night I took the trash out with my new friend and shared my story on the steps? That "friend" was Carole Loebs. That was the beginning of our friendship and the rest is history. If I had not trusted God to have that conversation with her, I'm convinced there's so much healing that would have never occurred in my life. God knows what's best. Let Him lead.

Paul even said that same life-giving, resurrection power that raised Jesus is alive inside of us. It's available to raise every dead thing in us to life.

Jesus said,

> *"But concerning the resurrection of the dead, have you not read what was spoken to you by God, saying, 'I am the God of Abraham, the God of Isaac, and the God of Jacob'? God is not the God of the dead, but of the living" (Matthew 22:31-32).*

Remember how Paul was changed from His old life on the road to Damascus? He was a Christ-hater, then became one who preached to Gentiles and wrote the majority of the New Testament. Forever changed by His encounter with Jesus, Paul had many great accomplishments but he said he *"counted all things loss for the excellence of the knowledge of Christ Jesus (his) Lord, for whom He had suffered the loss of all things, and counted them as rubbish, that he might gain Christ and be found in Him/ that he might know Him and the power of His resurrection" (Philippians 3:8-9a, 10a, emphasis mine).*

David Livingstone, a missionary to Africa in the 1800s, penned similar words, "I will place no value on anything I have or may possess except in relation to the kingdom of Christ." And the inscription upon the marble that marks his resting-place closes with his own words: "All I can say in my solitude is, may Heaven's rich blessing come down on every one—American, English, Turk—who will help to heal this open sore of the world."

The world and it's people are filled with open sores of fear, pain and guilt. I'm convinced the whole of our lives is a process of healing. Once we realize how broken we are, we attempt to find ways to be mended. Without the transforming power of Jesus, we have no hope of real restoration. We may heal a little here or there with doctor's visits and counseling, but really our Healer-God is the Only One who can mend us to true wholeness.

When a worm changes to a butterfly, it's a permanent change. Never again do we look at the butterfly and say, "Wow, look at that beautiful worm." No we marvel at its beauty as a butterfly. Why do so many of us mope around like the walking dead, even after we've been given a resurrected new soul? If it's guilt from the past, let it go. He has. Let Him breathe new, everlasting life, because He is *not a God of the dead but of the living.* A bunch of worms in need of transformation, He changes us. The walking dead come to life and we're free. We're finally beautiful butterflies.

> *...far above all principality and power and might and dominion, and every name that is named, not only in this age but also in that which is to come. And He put all things under His feet, and gave Him to be head over all things to the church, which is His body, the fullness of Him who fills all in all (Ephesians 1:21-23).*

David knew the power and authority of God in His own life. God saw his heart and had chosen and anointed him to be the next King of Israel. During a waiting period of years, God prepared David. Known as a man after God's heart, he trusted God. With a heart wide open, his faith in his all-powerful God was displayed for all to see when He faced the giant, Goliath.

Day after day for forty days and nights the Philistine giant marched out to challenge the Israelites. Who would face him? No one from the armies of Israel would volunteer. They were too afraid of being killed. David, only a shepherd boy, wasn't old enough to be in the battle. Out of obedience to his father, he was taking food to his older brothers in the army. He overheard the men talking about the giant. Imagine the heavy armor, sweat, testosterone, and the stench of those men and their attitudes toward David as he walked up on the scene.

After asking questions and being sent to speak with King Saul, David volunteered to fight the giant. He had killed lions and bears while tending sheep, so he was confident and ready. He knew God would provide and go before him.

Has God called you to do something greater? Do you feel stuck in a menial position? Realize right where you are is preparation ground for what is to come. I wouldn't be doing what I'm doing if God had not prepared and refined me in the wait. Without saying yes to God in the small things, I wouldn't have the opportunity to invest in women all over the world today. There's always a process. Again God knows what He's doing. Thankfully so because I certainly don't always know what I'm doing. I need Him. We all do!

David knew he needed God too, and he trusted. Because it was cumbersome, he wore no armor. With a sling and five smooth stones, he marched out in front of the giant. When Goliath saw David, that he was young and small in stature, he was insulted.

> *And the Philistine said to David, "Come to me, and I will give your flesh to the birds of the air and the beasts of the field!"*

> *Then David said to the Philistine, "You come to me with a sword, with a spear, and with a javelin. But I come to you in the name of the Lord of hosts, the God of the armies of Israel, whom you have defied. This day the Lord will deliver you into*

my hand, and I will strike you and take your head from you. And this day I will give the carcasses of the camp of the Philistines to the birds of the air and the wild beasts of the earth, that all the earth may know that there is a God in Israel. Then all this assembly shall know that the Lord does not save with sword and spear; for the battle is the Lord's, and He will give you into our hands" (1 Samuel 17:44-47).

David trusted the power and sovereignty of God to deliver him from the hand of this giant. Are you facing any giants that have placed a spirit of fear or oppression in your life? Face your giant with God-confidence. Though your giants may come with weapons meant to kill, you can stand in the face of them in the name of the Lord and say, *"The Lord will deliver you into my hand."* No matter how big your giant, *the battle is the Lord's.*

David didn't have much in his hand but he used what he had. What's in your hand right now? What little bit could you give, trusting God to deliver the rest? In whatever direction He decides to guide, you can be sure there's a good reason--if not many good reasons--for His decisions. What's keeping you from trusting the power and authority of Jesus? Are you giving Him full control to lead as He chooses?

Facing a giant of my own, I sat with a group of women congregated in a half circle. We all sported blue gowns with strings holding them together, (normally in the back but this time in the front). I had tied these on patients hundreds maybe thousands of times. This time I tied one on myself. I had been there three days prior, but they called me back to be rechecked. Peace overwhelmed as I prayed and released it to God. As He would have it, a close friend insisted on showing up to be by my side.

While taking me back, the sweet hospital staff reassured me that I would be leaving soon if the test showed nothing. Informed of the small possibility of needing the radiologist to take a closer look, I sat relieved that this would probably be over soon! A little uncomfortable to be letting it all hang out in the beautiful, light-blue, un-sequined gown, I heard the words, "Mrs. Douthit we need to have you come back for further testing." I could feel my tears churning in my eyes and throat. By the time my friend and I got to the next waiting area tears were forcing their way down my cheeks..

I thought, "This is really happening! In the next few minutes the trajectory of my life could be significantly different." I thought of people I had known and how terrified they must have been to actually be diagnosed and go through treatments. Now here I sat wondering. I felt her hand grab mine. My friend softly began praying peace and I felt the warmth of it wash over me. Thankful, the fast pace of my anxious heart began slowing. God kept reassuring me He was there and in control.

They called us in. It didn't occur to me that I would soon be lying partially topless in front of my friend until we were already in the room. When I was asked to lay down and remove my gown on that side, I thought, "Really Lord, really! What is going on here? This is humiliating! How different to be on this side of the gown." Then I thought, "Maybe God wants my friend in here with me for some reason. Maybe there's something I don't understand yet."

The stripping of the gown brought the stripping of pride. With my arm over my head, I was exposed as the ultrasound tech and radiologist checked. God spoke sweetly in that moment, "Rivera, I'm here. Either way you are going to be okay. I want you to understand how this feels so you can better relate to other women." He hushed my thoughts. He calmed my spirit. I knew no matter what the result, He had me.

The radiologist, who didn't look old enough to be out of high school, assured me there were no masses and nothing to be concerned about. Sigh. Relief. On the inside I was jumping up and down praising God! I knew how different this moment could have been, and I didn't take it for granted for a single second. I couldn't help but reflect and ache for all of those women with a different word from their doctor.

Before leaving the building, we sat down to talk. Thankful that she had taken the time to come and be with me, we began sharing our hearts. Then there it was! The knot in my throat. Realizing what God was doing, this whole chain of events was for another layer of emotional healing. I listened as she hopelessly shared, without mentioning names, her concern for someone who had lived a story similar to mine. She did not know my story and had no idea the similarities. Then her words faded into the background as God said, "Tell her."

He wanted me to share my story in full. I respected and loved my friend so much, but still there was fear of her judging or leaving if I shared. I questioned God, "Are You sure?" My heart pounded and I knew He was sure! Confession is difficult, but I allowed myself to be vulnerable. I had no choice. God said to do it. I had to. Risking rejection and exposing myself further, I told her.

She loved me through those regretful words, no questions asked. She said, "I'm so glad you told me. It gives me hope for this other woman." Our conversation led to growing intimacy in friendship. God knew what He was doing by exposing me in front of my friend! He was preparing me to be stripped again, this time to be transparent about my past. I'm not sure we're ever completely healed, until we're face to face with Jesus in heaven. For me, this was a deeper level of healing. My willingness to be vulnerable, in turn, helped her share. Our *Healer* Himself was clearly in our midst, gently cleaning the wounds of our exposed hearts.

Questions

1. Read 1 Samuel 16:1-13. What set David apart from his brothers to be the chosen king of Israel?

2. What's in your heart? Ask Holy Spirit to examine and do open heart surgery to remove anything that shouldn't be in your heart.

3. Maybe your heart is a mess and you feel embarrassed to let God see it. Realize He already sees it and He loves you anyway. Read: John 3:17

4. Perhaps your heart is an overflow of joy and thankfulness. How can you share what's in your heart with others? What are some ways you might share the love of Jesus and how He's changed your heart?

5. The heart gives life. Without the blood, the heart can't survive. God sent His only Son Jesus to die on a cross, shed His blood so we could have life. Is your heart happy and healthy?

Is it filled with the life of Jesus? Read Galatians 5:22-24. What should be the result of having Holy Spirit living in you? Does what's inside your heart reflect God or the world? Life or death? Invite Holy Spirit to saturate every part with HIs presence to make you full of life and more like Him.

6. Read Ezekiel 18:31-32. *Shuwb* is the Hebrew word for turn. Has there been a specific time in your life when you turned away from something? What was the result? List some ways you might turn the eyes of your heart more toward Jesus and away from things of this world?

7. Are you facing any giants that have led to a spirit of fear or oppression in your life? What is keeping you from trusting the power and authority of Jesus Christ? Are you giving God full control to lead as He chooses?

For soaking, listen to:

Bethel Music & Jeremy Riddle. "Fall Afresh" *The Loft Sessions*

Seven

Held

"The withered seed, with lack of form and attractiveness, will rise from the dust of the earth a beautiful flower." ~ Charles Spurgeon

His crying and silent screaming were too intense to let words through, and I knew something was terribly wrong. Waving and pointing to his hand he couldn't get words out to explain what had happened. Seeing it was reddened and beginning to swell, I was still unsure of what had happened. Asking questions, I made ice water to clean and sooth. As his hand soaked in the cold his words poured out to explain what had happened. Discovering the loose muffler while driving the old mower, he strapped it to prevent the rattling. Thinking it hadn't been turned on long enough to get hot, he grabbed the muffler.

Pain, regardless of whether it's physical or emotional, can take our breath away. In my late twenties I came home to North Carolina for a visit from California. Without a clue this would be our last visit, we sat on grandma's back porch stringing green beans. Hugging and sharing laughs I told Aunt Evelyn I would be having my first baby in a few months. A few days later she passed away unexpectedly while sleeping. Grief hit like a tidal wave. I couldn't speak, think, or begin to absorb what was happening. I was numb. The church filled to overflowing to celebrate her life, but I can't remember a single face. My heart was broken and the pain intense.

Trying to make sense of it all, I looked to God's Word. It said, *"in everything give thanks; for this is the will of God in Christ Jesus for you" (1 Thessalonians 5:18)*. I struggled with this, especially the *everything* part. How could I possibly be thankful for my Aunt Evelyn's passing? Since it said, *"in everything give thanks,* I reasoned that being thankful *in the midst of* rather than *for* her passing would suffice. But in Ephesians 5:20 Paul says to *"give thanks always for all things to God the Father in the name of our Lord Jesus Christ."* This verse didn't allow me to omit being thankful *for* my aunt's passing. *All things* included being thankful for her death.

With compassion and love, God orchestrated as only He could've, giving us treasured, unforgettable moments. He scheduled my two-week vacation, so I could see her one last time. He gently took her in her sleep so she didn't suffer. One of her sayings was, "I like to take the path of least resistance. It's a whole lot less stressful." And that she did! Sweetly and easily she slipped into the arms of *Love* and woke up in heaven. For that I was thankful. I knew it was God's will, and I rested in that. Was I thankful I no longer had my aunt? Of course not. That was a tough one. Only Jesus in me could work that out. *He* had to help me be thankful. Right before He was taken to the cross, he ate with the disciples.

> *And He took bread, gave thanks and broke it, and gave it to them, saying, "This is My body which is given for you; do this in remembrance of Me" (Luke 22:19).*

Knowing the agony and pain He would soon face, He gave thanks. He showed us by example how to give thanks *for* and *in* our darkest hour. If Jesus could be thankful for the cross, He could help me give thanks for my aunt dying.

Being thankful doesn't mean it makes sense. I still don't understand it. Being thankful didn't take away the pain, which (like Hunter with the muffler) left me unable to process or even speak. Aunt Evelyn passed thirteen years ago and I still am taken back at the most inopportune moments, finding myself tearful and overwhelmed by loss. But I have hope and confidence through Jesus. There had to have been a good reason, and one day I'll see her again.

AMAZING GRACE

When the phone rang near midnight, my heart sank. Instinctively I knew it wasn't good news. Though it's more comfortable to think tragedies can only happen to other people, I knew better. Fact is none of us are immune. Disasters can happen to anyone at any moment. Unexpected and heart-wrenching, a cousin who lit up every room with her contagious smile tucked her five babies into bed for the last time. Her six-month-old won't remember and her husband and family were left to pick up the pieces.

My churning stomach over her passing reminded me of the pain and grief I'd witnessed so often while working in Critical Care. Death is the most dreaded thing in life. Maybe it's not dying as much as the process of dying we fear. Maybe it's our separation from loved ones or just that there's so little we understand about it. Our fear of the unknown suffocates. When the life of someone we love is ripped away we are devastated, wanting to ask why or blame God. After all, He controls everything. Couldn't He have prevented this?

My heart asks why. What possible purpose could there be in allowing a 29-year old to be taken from her babies? What in the world? The Father's voice echoes back, "It's sin in the world. That's *what*. Remember the garden and how death is a result of sin? It's My timing and I have a right to bring My children home with Me when I please. Remember I Am God? I see things you can't see."

Death is ultimately the result of sin in this fallen world. While I know this with my head my breaking heart still doesn't get it. Can we continue on with acceptance and faith and stand with unwavering trust that, even at our very darkest hour, God is good? When all seems stripped from our hands, still there is no evil in God. His intent is always for our good. Why doesn't it feel like it? It hurts so bad we can hardly breathe. How could God possibly love or care if He's taken everything we love most, prematurely? How can this be love? Will we trust it is? Will we be able to resist the bitterness trying to take root in our souls, or will it slither its way in slowly?

With so much injustice and wickedness in the world: genocide, sex trafficking, and so many other crimes against humanity, why take a beautiful, innocent and loving young woman away from her family? Do these wicked people really deserve to live? How does this make sense? Again His patient response, "Those people who don't deserve to live are no different from you. Every human has sinned Rivera. I died for the sins of the whole world, not just for a few. She is mine and it's simply her time to be home with Me."

He knows our thoughts before we think them. Doesn't He know our grief and pain before we experience it? He knows pain and loss, the most profound. Our Father gave his Son over to death for our sake, so surely He knows. He would have to. No doubt He loves us and empathizes with our losses.

As if she had been given a calming drug, her mama told how she didn't want to see her daughter's body lying in a casket. But as she talked, it was apparent that something or Someone beyond her-self had taken over. All my life I heard my preacher-grandpa say, "*His grace is sufficient, and His strength is made perfect in our weakness.*" Is this what he meant? After all, this is how we "*glory in our infirmities, so Christ's power can rest on us,*" right? Resting in the sufficiency of

God's grace is how we praise in the storm. When we don't know how to go on, each breath in sync with His, He carries us on. Without His presence, we can't find it in ourselves to praise or give thanks in *all* things.

> *I can do all things through Christ who strengthens me (Philippians 4:13).*

Her mama said seeing her there in that casket almost made it easier to accept. She said, "I knew *Grace* was with us. We are in the presence of *Grace.*" And I knew it too, as I watched her.

I remembered experiencing the same *Grace* when Aunt Evelyn died. I recall my grandma saying she had seen one of everyone in her life put in the earth,--mama, daddy, aunts, uncles, grandparents, cousins, and even her husband--but burying her daughter was the worst. Then my grandma stood with dignity and strength, held by *Grace,* as dirt poured over Aunt Evelyn's casket. Grandma knew Him. She spent time with Him. We all witnessed His sufficiency covering her. When we seemed to need it most, we experienced it too. His hush. Her mama's calm showed it like Grandma's. It was evidence of *Grace* declaring to everyone listening and watching how God was present. Not just in that moment, but God's Spirit in her all the time.

How can we know for sure we know Him and He knows us? That we're in Him and He's in us? The one who leaned in to Jesus penned it best, *"Now he who keeps His commandments abides in Him, and He in him. And by this we know that He abides in us, by the Spirit whom He has given us" (1 John 3:24).* When we go through a crisis, it is well with our souls and peace like a river overwhelms because of His Spirit in us.

It was the Spirit living inside her that washed over her with peace. She stood in the darkness of her life preparing to bury her daughter. Pressing in to the deepest place in her soul she worshipped and praised Jesus for grace.

When we can't breathe, how can we possibly praise? Are we praising already as we attempt to empty our tormented hearts to Him in all honesty? Praise is after all about communicating with God. It's about glorifying Him in every facet of our lives. Isn't it possible to exalt Him in our suffering? When we walk through heartbreak with dignity and unexplainable peace we reflect His glory and in this we praise. When we stand in His sufficiency, though we're broken, we honor Him. So in our darkest hours we love Him by pleading, by crying, by leaning in to Him who understands. We can't fathom and can't help but ask why. Our sincere cries in our pain to the One who knows us may be as a pleasing to Him as a sweet song. The more we pour out tears like a drink offering, the more we glory in the One who knows us best.

THE RIVER

I despised going to sleep as a child for fear of missing something. Perhaps the only thing that disturbs me about dying is that I might miss what's going on with my children, future grandchildren, family, and friends. But I'm convinced what's waiting for me there far exceeds what I have and know here.

Growing up, my grandparents were our neighbors, and I would sneak to their house as often as possible. Sitting at my preacher-grandpa's feet asking questions about his life and the Bible was one of my favorite things to do. Grandma told the best stories, and taught me to cook and quilt, not that I'm great at either today. Once for punishment, I was banned from visiting their house for an entire week. My world nearly ended.

While I was in college grandpa passed away. In my early thirties, my beloved grandma was diagnosed with Alzheimer's. Her entire life she had the wonderful ability to make every individual seem like the most important person in the world. Her church family called her *grandma,* and she knew each and every one by name. She loved to gracefully move through a room, lighting up every space. As she was getting closer to the end of her life, she worried God couldn't use her. I assured her, "As long as you have breath grandma, He's using you." He did. Although she couldn't always find her way to her bedroom, she never forgot names or how to make people feel special.

In the weeks leading to her passing, I prayed God would take her home to be with Him quickly and peacefully. It was probably the hardest prayer I'd ever prayed, but I knew she was miserable. Within a few weeks the hours were drawing near to her passing. She would see and speak to her brothers who had passed on to be with Jesus years prior. She spoke of being at the edge of the river. Having never learned to swim, she was afraid to cross. I couldn't help but get this image of her soul being between two worlds, her earthly home and her home in heaven. It reminded me of this Psalm,

> *There is a river whose streams shall make glad the city of God, The holy place of the tabernacle of the Most High. God is in the midst of her, she shall not be moved; God shall help her, just at the break of dawn (Psalm 46:4-5).*

As she neared passing from one side of *the river* to the other, I assured her she had nothing to fear. Jesus would be with her. I promised He would hold her hand and so would I. Family and church friends gathered. The outpouring of love was evidence of the life she had lived. Being from a musical family, we gathered around her bed and sang hymns a cappella. She was unable to open her eyes and verbally unresponsive, but we heard her trying to hum the tune with us. What a beautiful display of His splendor as she worshiped in her dying moments.

She breathed her last breaths and I saw the glory of the Lord. With spiritual eyes, I saw my grandma's spirit body leave her physical body. In the arms of *Love,* I'm certain He picked her up and carried her across the river. In that moment, she was more alive than ever! In all my years as a nurse, I had never seen death through such spiritual eyes. Grandma passed away on Easter Sunday night. Such an honor it was to hold her hand as she met Jesus face to face.

> *For now we see in a mirror, dimly, but then face to face. Now I know in part, but then I shall know just as I also am known (1 Corinthians 13:12).*

Just as we are given physical life and an everlasting soul by the power of the living God, we are given over to death to be made truly alive through our glorified bodies. All are the power of Divine sovereignty. We know in those moments of life and death, only a God with the capacity to give and take away is in our midst.

WHEN LEAST EXPECTED

We stopped off at a little Podunk gas station in South Carolina to use the restroom. From the outside, we weren't sure how safe or clean it was, but we knew our bladders gave us no choice. The only other option was to stop on the side of the road and use the woods. Both seemed creepy but we opted for the one with a toilet. How were we to know there would be a line for this dark, disgusting, single toilet restroom? Squeezing my legs together and dancing, we waited and waited.

The lady in front of us seemed overly patient. I thought, "She must not need to go that bad." Trying to remain calm I turned to my friend,

"Goodness, I can't imagine what could be taking so long! The whites of my eyes must be turning yellow by now."

After fifteen minutes, still no one had come out of this restroom. Growing more impatient by the minute, I asked the lady in front of me, "Are we sure there's someone in there?"

She said, "Yes. When they come out, you're welcome to go before me."

I said, "No, it's ok. You've been waiting longer than I have. You should go ahead."

As the door opened, and I realized there were two women in the bathroom. The one with white hair and a face worn by years had her hands clinched tight around the walker in front of her. She slowly moved through the doorway with the sweetest grin. The lady waiting turned to me and said, "Sorry it took so long. It normally takes a while for my aunt. She has to have someone help her."

I managed to keep my composure until she left, then unstoppable tears flooded. I felt ridiculous for being impatient, for crying in the middle of this convenience store, and for letting myself go so long without peeing. About to wet my pants, I was a hot mess! During that wait, I had felt an array of emotions but this was not one I expected.

As the woman moved toward me with her walker, I pictured my grandma. I had helped her in and out of more bathrooms than I could count. What I wouldn't give to help her again. I remembered the grief when she passed. Alone in her house, pressing my face into her hand-made quilt, I smelled her again. Tears I had held in for months finally exploded as I laid across her bed.

She died over five years ago and it still catches me. Grief ebbs and flows when I least expect it, hitting like an ocean wave from behind. Revisiting my Aunt Evelyn's kitchen... seeing Laura's number in my phone... visiting with Ann's family... seeing my aunt after the loss of her son. All reminders of significant losses.

"Good grief!" Whoever invented that saying? As bad as it feels, grief actually *is* a good thing. It's a healthy thing. It's a healing thing. It comes and goes. Oh it looks a little different with time. Intensity and frequency become less through the years, but it's still grief. Just when we think it's over the wave raises and hits from behind again.

HOPE RISES

Tangibly and intimately surprised by *Grace*, my dear friend Lisa Kelley wrote,

> "I surprised Mom at work one evening to take her to dinner. It was one of those perfect nights where the conversation was upbeat. Mom was on her way to Savannah the next day with some girlfriends for a much deserved week's vacation. I was thrilled for her. After the last bite of our cheesecake, I gave mom a hug and told her I loved her. And for some reason I stopped to watch her walk to her car and drive away waving and smiling. I didn't know then how precious that moment really was.

> The following week, while packing to come home from her Savannah vacation, my mother collapsed in the hotel room. A blood clot traveled into her lung, and she stopped breathing and died almost instantly. I was on the phone with her friends, while the medical crew was trying to revive her. And I was on the phone when she passed away. In that moment, I felt

hopelessness and desperation that I never knew existed. I asked God to take me. I prayed that I too would stop breathing. The pain was too great. The prayers of some faithful believers and the love of my Savior carried me through those perilous hours. The physical pain I was experiencing was lifted as a veil of peace and love miraculously passed over me. The Creator of the universe, of every star in the sky and every living being on earth, was holding me in the palm of His hand. He was answering prayers on my behalf. It was a feeling I will never forget.

Later that week I had to empty the suitcase that my mother was packing when she died. I held her clothing to my face and tried to breathe her in. I held her sweaters and wrapped the arms around my neck in hope of feeling her in the embrace. I dipped my fingers in her moisturizing cream and caressed my face with her blush brush hoping to see her face looking back in the mirror. I longed to hear her voice tell me about her trip. I decided since it was the last thing her human hands touched I would keep mom's suitcase in my closet. The luggage wasn't pretty. It was olive green with lime trim which are my two least favorite colors. But mom said it was different than everyone else's so that no one could steal it at the airport. She was so practical since she rarely flew anywhere.

The suitcase stayed in my closet for a couple years. I considered donating it to a worthy charity once but was not ready to let it go. The following year, I was fortunate enough to be picked for a team of counselors and students to travel to Uganda to work with women and children who were affected by the war. I chose to take mom's suitcase so I could take a piece of her with me.

We each packed two large suitcases with clothing, food and ministry supplies. When we were packing to come home, most on the team decided to leave all their clothing and luggage behind for the ministry to use. I knew that leaving mom's suitcase was the right thing to do. It was time to let it go. Before I walked away from it for the last time, I brushed my fingers across the lime green zipper, smiled, and said goodbye. I knew that Mom's suitcase had a higher purpose.

Months passed and I was excited the ministry founder was coming to the states for a fundraising campaign. She was asked to speak at churches in many states, including Charlotte, NC, near my hometown. I traveled to see her and help her bring awareness to the victims of sex trafficking in Africa. I was eager to help her set-up the display of handmade African jewelry and crafts. She pointed under a draped table to a suitcase that was full of jewelry made by my dear sisters in Uganda who worked tirelessly to support themselves.

The room was dimly lit, but as I walked closer to the table I stopped and gasped. Of all the suitcases that were left behind in Uganda, mom's suitcase was chosen to carry this precious cargo. My eyes welled with tears of joy not only for having the opportunity to see mom's suitcase again, but also for the promise that it represented. Even in my most desperate hours, when I didn't want to breathe or live, God promised that He would never leave me or forsake me. When I didn't know how I would survive without her, God promised that there was hope for my future.

I never considered asking for mom's suitcase that day. I know God honored my sacrifice by allowing me to see it one more time. As far as I know, it is still being used by the ministry. Even though it's not attractive, it is sturdy. And its color makes it distinct enough not to get stolen at the airport so the precious jewelry it carries will more likely reach its intended destination. God honors his promises. Sometimes He does it by offering peace during a time of despair, a trip to a foreign land to help those less fortunate, or sometimes through an old suitcase."

This is what it is to have God in our business. This is what it is to know He knows everything there is to know about us: every day, every hair on our heads, every heartache. It's what it means to be held by God and face to face in His presence, like Moses who wanted to see Him in all His glory. No one could see God's face and live, so God's hands covered Moses in the cleft of the rock while He passed by. It wasn't until He passed that Moses was able to see Him from behind. As Holy hands covered the rock Moses couldn't see, but God's presence was closer than ever.

In our darkest, loneliest, most painful moments we get to know Him like never before. In those times of mixed up grief and questioning our star-hanging God, who held Himself on a cross for our sin, is holding us. In our suffering He's closer than ever. He won't let go!

It's what Paul meant when he said he considered every great accomplishment in his life rubbish compared to *"knowing Him (Jesus) and the power of His resurrection, and the fellowship of His sufferings" (Philippians 3:10).* It's deep pain that brings opportunity to know Jesus more intimately and be found in Him. Slowly transforming us, it's a sure process of becoming more like Him. Naked in our sufferings before God, we like Moses, are in His presence and *"we all, with open face beholding as in a glass the glory of the Lord, are changed into the same image from glory to glory, even as by the Spirit of the Lord" (2 Corinthians 3:18).*

A refining so perfect and pure, pain brings us to our knees in absolute submission and complete reverence as we are held by the Almighty.

Tears of sorrow flow, cleansing the soul, and He wipes them dry. The Comforter comforts. Changing us. Slowly. It's intimacy with the Living God.

Questions

1. When was the last time you experienced pain? Was it physical, spiritual, or emotional? What affect did it have on you?

2. Read Psalm 116:15. Have you ever experienced the death of someone close or significant loss? Who or what did you lose? Was the loss expected or sudden? How did you cope? Why do you suppose death of the saints is precious to God?

3. Grief is normal, necessary, and different for every individual. When was the last time you felt grief? Did you feel bad or uncomfortable to allow yourself to grieve? What did it look like for you?

4. When you don't know how to go on in a storm or in deep grief, do you run to the embrace of Grace or try run away from God's presence? Do you know why you do what you do?

5. Read Job 1:13-22. What happened to Job's servants and family? What were Job's words toward God? Is it difficult to glorify God in your trials? Read Ephesians 5:20 1 Thessalonians 5:18. Are you able to find a way to give thanks for ALL things?

6. In the midst of trials, do you have difficulty trusting God? Why or why not?

For soaking, listen to:

Laura Hackett. "You Satisfy My Soul" *You Satisfy My Soul-Single*

Eight

Extravagant Worship

"Every form of worship lacking sincerity of the heart is nothing but a solemn sham and an impudent mockery of the Majesty in heaven." ~ Charles Spurgeon

A man in Vietnam was making a delivery. His route required him to travel through rubber tree farms. When his motorcycle ran out of gas, he was desperate. With no filling stations or people nearby to ask for help, he began to pray. He believed with everything in him Jesus would rescue. Traveling with one gallon of water, he heard Holy Spirit say, "Fill the tank with your gallon of water." Realizing this could ruin the engine, he did it anyway. He turned the key and the motorcycle started. Traveling another seventy kilometers, he safely reached his destination.

If Jesus could turn water into quality wine, why wouldn't He be able to turn water into gasoline?

> *Jesus Christ is the same yesterday, today, and forever (Hebrews 13:8).*

If He hasn't changed it stands to reason He would still be doing miracles today. Christians in other countries who so often have been persecuted for their faith seem to get this. God will always be the God of miracles. In our *self*-driven and *self*-sufficient world of abundance, this is difficult for most

Americans to believe. God is in control. He can and will do miracles if we believe. That is worth getting excited about! It's worth sharing. *He* is worth sharing. Jesus is worthy of it all: reaching our hands toward heaven, singing our songs, playing our instruments, making a joyful noise, and giving praise where praise is due! Our Creator, miracle-working God is worthy! Miracles often hinge on our adoration of the One who still can and will do the miraculous. Worship moves the heart of God so much He created music-making stars. God questioned Job and pointed out he wasn't there at creation,

> *Where were you when I laid the foundations of the earth? Tell Me, if you have understanding. Who determined its measurements? Surely you know! Or who stretched the line upon it? To what were its foundations fastened? Or who laid its cornerstone, When the morning stars sang together, And all the sons of God shouted for joy? ~Job 38:4-7*

God gives a glimpse of what it was like when He created. Not at all surprising, scientists have discovered that stars really do sing! The only way human ears can hear them is by artificially boosting their sounds. This points out God's position of worthiness and authority as Creator. He can hear His stars singing without an "artificial boost." They were clearly created for His glory and enjoyment, not ours.

Given a vision of the scene around the throne of God, John wrote about how praises never cease in heaven.

> *The four living creatures, each having six wings, were full of eyes around and within. And they do not rest day or night, saying:*
>
> *"Holy, holy, holy,*

Lord God Almighty,

Who was and is and is to come!"

Whenever the living creatures give glory and honor and thanks to Him who sits on the throne, who lives forever and ever, the twenty-four elders fall down before Him who sits on the throne and worship Him who lives forever and ever, and cast their crowns before the throne, saying:

"You are worthy, O Lord,

To receive glory and honor and power;

For You created all things,

And by Your will they exist and were created" (Revelation 4:8-11).

If God loves hearing the stars and heavenly creatures around His throne sing praises, how much must He adore our praises? In high school and college, I had the joy of singing in ensembles of less than twenty and large choirs of hundreds. Privileged to sing in two different famous Cathedrals in my lifetime, I've also had the privilege as an adult to lead hundreds in worship. I've been an attendee in coliseum settings with thousands of voices worshiping together.

Besides a breath-taking view of God's creation, to me there's nothing on earth quite as beautiful as thousands of voices and hands raised in worship. A little slice of heaven, it reminds me of these verses from Revelation. When worshipping in song, I often imagine the angels in heaven singing with me or vice versa. The thought of joining in with the heavenly choir excites me. Imagine millions of voices making a beautiful sound for the glory and honor of God. (And interestingly there won't be fighting in heaven over musical preference). We'll all just be praising, and it will be glorious.

King Jehoshaphat (King J for short) knew the power of praising our Most High God. The day before the battle God used Jahaziel to speak to the people including King J. He told them this battle was not their's but God's. He encouraged them to position themselves and watch God save.

> *Jehoshaphat bowed down with his face to the ground, and all the people of Judah and Jerusalem fell down in worship before the Lord. Then some Levites from the Kohathites and Korahites stood up and praised the Lord, the God of Israel, with a very loud voice./ (The next morning) After consulting the people, Jehoshaphat appointed men to sing to the Lord and to praise him for the splendor of his holiness as they went out at the head of the army, saying:*
>
> *"Give thanks to the Lord,*
>
> *for his love endures forever."*
>
> *As they began to sing and praise, the Lord set ambushes against the men of Ammon and Moab and Mount Seir who were invading Judah, and they were defeated (2 Chronicles 20:18-19, 21-22, emphasis mine).*

Before the battle, King J sought the Lord through prayer. He proclaimed a fast throughout Judah. If you've never fasted, you might consider it. What better way to worship God than by denying ourselves something temporal in pursuit of the eternal? It's a way to humble ourselves and press in closer to Holy.

Face down in humility on the day of the battle, the king led the army in worship. The heart of God was moved by their hearts of worship for Him. *Salvation* went before them and won the battle. They stood and saw the deliverance of the Lord.

Have you ever faced a battle and had no idea how you would get through it? Jesus is big enough to win our battles. He came to save. While on the cross taking His last breaths, the King of all kings and Salvation of the world won the battle for us. He said, "It is finished." The battle was over. He conquered our sin, then conquered death when He rose again. Take your battles to the cross of Jesus. He's in the business of winning.

DANNY

Over eight years had passed since we lived in California. I wondered what might have happened to him. My husband's family had known Danny's for years. I remembered seeing him pirouette on and off the sidewalks in the neighboring town. With hands held high, he would yell, "Jesus is faithful! Jesus is faithful!" In the years we lived there, admittedly, there were times I wondered what would possess a man to so zealously dance on the streets. I thought, "Maybe he's lost his mind or on drugs."

During one of my last visits to California, I settled in at a local coffee shop with my favorite latte to write while they were still open. On the opposite end of the bench from where I sat, a man spoke to me, "Hey, how are you this evening?"

Halfheartedly I replied, "Fine, thanks." I continued what I was doing, trying to make it clear I was uninterested in idle chit-chat.

He went on enthusiastically, "It's really nice weather out there, isn't it?

I thought, "That's a likely line." Smiling I said, "Yes it is," and went straight back to writing. I know. I know it wasn't very nice, but I was pushed for time. I was staying with my in-laws who didn't have wireless internet, so I was hurrying before they closed.

Two young guys sat down across from him. Their meeting seemed planned. The tall one was wearing a black shirt with skulls. With his Bible in front of him, the gentleman beside me smiled as they joined him. When they sat down the tall one said, "I have a question for you. What is a God?"

He told them there are many gods (little g) but one true God (big G). He explained how things in this world become the object of people's worship and become little g's—fame, money, jobs, people, food, self. But there's only one true God who says, "There shall be no other gods before me."

> He said, "Jesus is the Way, the Truth, and the Life, and no one can come to the Father except through Him."

With every question, He gave a detailed scriptural explanation. I had never heard anyone teach God's Word so boldly with that clarity and confidence, without opening the Bible. It was apparent He knew God's Word. It was hidden in his heart. Excitedly he spoke, *"Jesus was in the beginning... Through Him all things were made that were made... "*

I sat on the edge of my seat. I wanted to cheer him on! I spoke to the guy with the skull shirt and said, "For whatever it's worth, I can't help but hear this conversation and everything he's telling you is the truth!"

They questioned and he continued, "This world is filled with darkness... Jesus is the light of the world... We are to be light in the darkness, and Jesus helps us do that... God is a good God, and He wants all to come to repentance and life. Our Father can't have anything to do with sin, but He wants a relationship with us. He made a way through Jesus. Jesus died for our sin. We all have a choice to accept or reject Him."

About thirty minutes into this evangelical question and answer, He began sharing from personal experience. He had me when he said, "I've never had many friends. At one time in my life, it really bothered me. But over the years, I've learned as long as I have Jesus, I'm never alone. I'm completely fulfilled. He's all I need. He's all any of us need."

My heart sank to my knees. Here I had sat down to write about my love for Jesus, yet I had snubbed this sweet guy who just needed someone to talk to. How wrong was I? It made me sick. Meanwhile those guys, who apparently had never encountered Jesus until that moment, listened to every word he said.

He went on, "I danced for the San Francisco Ballet and traveled all over the world. I got to see some amazing things. But all the beauty and riches in the world don't compare to knowing Jesus and having a relationship with Him."

"The San Francisco Ballet? Could it be Danny?" I wondered.

The guys apologetically had to leave. He asked for their names so he could pray for them. Apparently they didn't know each other at all. No one had planned this meeting except God. He turned to me after they left and said, "Thank you. You are an encourager. I knew you were praying for me as I was talking to those guys. Will you please pray for them?" He reached for my hand, "What's your name?"

Shaking his hand I said, "My name is Rivera, and yours?"

He replied, "Daniel. You know, like in the lion's den?"

I smiled, "Yes. I know Daniel."

149

He said, "Humility is beautiful. You know, you are beautiful." What he said next penetrated my heart. Jesus Himself may as well have been speaking in that moment. He smiled and said, "You know Rivera, we can have the Bible memorized and can minister to people all day long, but if we don't love none of it means a thing." I knew this truth from 1 Corinthians 13, but I obviously needed to be reminded. It's so simple yet so easy to forget, isn't it?

I smiled. "Daniel I agree with you. Thank you for that truth." I silently prayed, "Lord, I did not extend love and grace toward Danny earlier. Please forgive me!"

Then I asked, "How can I pray specifically for you Daniel?"

"Pray that I remain pure and steadfast. I've messed up a lot. Pray that I finish well. I just want God to look at me and say 'well done!' Yes, just pray that I finish well," he replied.

God used Danny, a misunderstood ballet dancer with few friends, to speak truth over me that night. He did it in love, and I experienced church right there over my laptop and coffee. Daniel loved me through my unlovely, self-centered behavior. I left feeling I had been nearer God. He was being the church. He loved like Jesus. He had encountered *Grace* firsthand, like I had. Now, on the other side of my own story of being wooed back into the arms of Love, I understood Danny's enthusiasm. I knew firsthand what would cause this man to pirouette on the sidewalks, yelling, "Jesus is faithful." He had been called to come closer. Healed from his past, he had been set free to run. Dancing with the Divine, he was a beautiful display of worship!

More than songs, worship is the way we live. It's what happens when we come closer to *Love*. Danny was in love with *Love,* and his life and words to others a song of praise. He wasn't worried about what people would think of him. He spoke about his love for his Savior with passion and boldness mixed with a dash of gentleness. It's what Paul was referring to in Colossians 4:5-6.

> *"Walk in wisdom toward those who are outside, redeeming the time." Colossians 4:5*

The Greek word for time in this verse is *kairos* (kahee-ross), and it means "opportune time, set time, appointed time, due time, definitive time, seasonable time, proper time for action." It describes a "kind or quality of time." Another word for time is *chronos,* which "denotes extent or quantity of time." The time Paul is speaking of is kairos, or quality of time. When we walk or speak in wisdom with others, God may be redeeming something for them. God wants our times with Him and others to be quality. Every word we speak should be words worthy of being spoken. With His wisdom guiding they will be.

Though we should use the time He's given us wisely, I love this verse because it indicates lost time isn't a huge deal to God. Time to us and time to Him are very different. If we give our "to do" lists to Him, first thing each day, He will manage our time better than we could alone. My friend Cammie Wilson once said,

> "When we give our time, schedule and obligations to Him, He supernaturally gives us above and beyond everything we need to complete the task! He's that powerful!"

He's a flawless orchestrator. I understand this isn't logical, but dealing with God isn't always. He's bigger than our "lists." He's beyond our human reasoning. As we surrender to His scheduling and agenda, He will maneuver the events of our days. When our times are given over to Him, God helps complete everything we have to do and more.

Being a business owner and manager, my husband is a list guy. Without a plan, he feels lost. In the last couple of years, God has been teaching David to give his lists and plans to Him. As my husband has let go, he's seen God in his days. He's watched Him work miracles to manage his work schedule. He's seen God provide more financially with less time invested.

God can take a little bit and turn it into a lot. Small in quantity becomes large in quality with Jesus. A Redeemer of time, He gives back what's been lost and then some. Maybe you thought He called you to something but you never followed through or had a chance to do it. He can restore what's been lost. It may not look the way you thought it would or should, but God is a Redeemer of lost things...time, things, even people.

Worship can be as simple as handing over our lists, callings, and times to God. It can be as easy as saying I trust You with everything that I am and everything I have. In the writing process for this book, every minute of every single day was valuable. When people would call to chat, send a message wanting to meet for coffee, or ask me to do something for ministry, I had to politely say no. Staying focused on what God said to do during this time was part of my worship.

Before writing I would often start by thanking God for who He is, then pray Romans 12:1, "Lord Jesus, *I offer* (my time, my thoughts, my words), *my body a living sacrifice, holy, acceptable, and pleasing to You, which is my reasonable act of worship."* This is a tough one, I know. Presenting our bodies to God as a sacrifice of praise isn't always easy. Our *body is a temple of the Holy Spirit,* so treating ourselves with respect and dignity is part of being a good steward of what God has entrusted to us. Loving the body He gave us can be as simple as drinking enough water, eating healthy, and exercising. Honestly, praising Him through song, writing, and speaking are much easier for me than avoiding dark chocolate and diet soda. Let's not even discuss coffee.

Looking in the mirror and realizing we are beautiful just the way He made us is God-honoring. My sweet friend Margaret who is seventy something going on twenty something always says,

> "Each day is a gift. I wake up every morning and thank God for another day. Then, no matter how rough I look, I stare in the mirror and say to myself, 'You are beautiful, because you are God's masterpiece."

This says, "I love your creation God, even if it is imperfect me. Because You made me, I choose to love me." A lifestyle of worship is not necessarily about giving up things. More than anything, God desires hearts after His.

Each day as I wrote, I specifically prayed, "Jesus, give me daily manna in this time." Basically I was asking Him to give me just enough to complete the task for that day, no less and no more. I wanted Him to give what *He knew* I needed, not what *I thought* I needed. He did. Every word written was poured out as an offering of praise and thanksgiving back to Him.

Maybe yours isn't writing a book, but whatever it is it's obviously valuable. Otherwise He wouldn't want you to do it. Giving it to Him with a willing and determined heart is worship.

> *Let your speech always be with grace, seasoned with salt, that you may know how you ought to answer each one (Colossians 4:5-6).*

When my grandma was still living at home after being diagnosed with Alzheimer's, she canned tomato juice. When we made soup with it, we realized she had accidentally over-salted the juice. We threw the soup away because it wasn't edible.

Similar with our words, we can become so zealous as Christians we ruin the conversation or turn people off to God. Some pastors and church-goers are guilty of this. I have a close family member who, as a teenage boy, sat in the back of the church with friends. During the ending portion of the service a well-meaning (I think) woman went back to tell he and his friends they needed to go forward to "get saved." He left that day and never went back to church. He's now in his sixties. This woman did not let *Grace* season her words. We have to realize we are not the Holy Spirit. God is the One who convicts and saves, not us. Know your audience, pray for Holy Spirit wisdom and choose every word wisely. Season your words with just enough saltiness or *Grace* to taste good.

We could've added water to my grandma's over-salted tomato juice and it may have tasted similar to soup. Watered down, it would've been a much weaker tasting tomato soup. Instead of being overly salty, some churches take it to the opposite extreme. Due to the scars many churches have left with their extreme saltiness, other churches have tried to compensate by watering down the message of Jesus. Many of them speak truth, it's just weakened with compromise. Jesus wants us to stand firm on the truth of His Word and worship Him in the way we deal with people. We represent Him with our time, bodies, and words at all times.

Danny tastefully shared the good news of Jesus and part of his own story. Those guys in the coffee shop will probably never forget their conversation with him, and I know I won't. We worship when we share our stories, our God encounters, and witness to others of His greatness. Don't underestimate the power of simply sharing how Jesus has changed your life.

POURED OUT

Jesus went to dine with a Pharisee whose thoughts and words were not seasoned with Grace. A sinful woman from the city knew Jesus was there. Bringing an expensive bottle of fragrant oil, she began humbly washing His feet with her hair and tears. Kissing His feet, she anointed them with her perfume.

> *Now when the Pharisee who had invited Him saw this, he spoke to himself, saying, "This Man, if He were a prophet, would know who and what manner of woman this is who is touching Him, for she is a sinner" (Luke 7:39).*

I've always wondered how this Pharisee, Simon, knew her. Was he (or his wife) the town gossip? Had he personally encountered her? We're not given her name or the nature of her sin, but one popular belief is that it may have been sexual. Only God knows her sin and Simon's dealings with her. The thoughts he had about her while she kissed Jesus' feet were harsh, so he had at least heard of her bad reputation. Simon, thinking Jesus couldn't possibly be a prophet, had no idea he was in the presence of the God-Who-Sees. He was sitting across the room from Holy.

Jesus saw Simon's heart. Hearing his thoughts and seasoned with grace, Jesus politely called him out. He told a parable of a creditor and two debtors. One debtor owed more than the other but both were pardoned what they owed. Jesus asked Simon which of the two men in debt loved the most. Simon rightly answered, guessing the one who had been forgiven the most debt.

> *He (Jesus) said to him, "You have rightly judged." Then He turned to the woman and said to Simon, "Do you see this woman? I entered your house; you gave Me no water for My feet, but she has washed My feet with her tears and wiped*

them with the hair of her head. You gave Me no kiss, but this woman has not ceased to kiss My feet since the time I came in. You did not anoint My head with oil, but this woman has anointed My feet with fragrant oil. Therefore I say to you, her sins, which are many, are forgiven, for she loved much. But to whom little is forgiven, the same loves little" (Luke 7:43b-47).

Providing a basin for washing feet, greeting with a kiss, and anointing the head with common oil were all custom at this time when having friends or guests over for dinner. Jesus points out how Simon thought to do none of these, but this woman had done them all.

In Jesus' presence she was overcome with emotion. Her regret over her sin was uncontainable. In the presence of Love she emptied herself at His feet. The eyes that had previously been an inlet for sin now poured tears to cleanse her Savior's feet. Hair that had probably been pulled up and adorned, now hung straight hiding her face and served as a drying towel. In the presence of Holy, lips that weren't worthy to touch His face kissed his feet in reverence.

With no name mentioned, she may have felt lonely and invisible. When a girl carries a bad reputation she normally doesn't have many friends. Most of her interactions were ones of being judged. Jesus knew her. He designed her. God in human flesh had memorized every detail of this woman's life. He understood what circumstances led her to sin.

I heard a story about a doctor who treated a woman on a regular basis. He was a gynecologist, and she persistently had female problems relating to her lifestyle and choices. He was prompted by Holy Spirit to talk to her. During one of her visits the doctor went into the hallway to pray for the right words. He went in and humbly asked, "What happened?" Through tears she shared. He listened and responded with compassion and love. In that moment she realized he saw beyond her physical body. He saw through to the pain of her past. He saw her. He cared.

Jesus saw beyond this woman's sin. He saw her love for Him spill out. Rolling down the top of His feet, her perfume was the most expensive thing she owned. She brought her most valuable possessions, her alabaster jar of fragrant oil and her heart. When we're in love, we trust the one we love with our heart and everything most meaningful, don't we? God wants us to trust Him with those things most valuable to us. He wants our hearts. She laid her past and her future at His feet. Experiencing His love, compassion and healing power, all she could do was worship and weep.

On some days, especially if I'm hormonal, I cry about everything. A mere thought of what Jesus has done in my life and my eyes leak liquid joy and thankfulness over His love for me. Tears are special and often hard earned. Don't be afraid of them.

> Then He said to her, "Your sins are forgiven."

> And those who sat at the table with Him began to say to themselves, "Who is this who even forgives sins?"

> Then He said to the woman, "Your faith has saved you. Go in peace" (Luke 7:48-50).

Facing judgment from a house full of religious-spirited people, this woman came to drench Jesus with an offering of humble adoration. He forgave and sent her away in peace. She had been forgiven of much, so her capacity *for love* and *to love* was greater than most. Uncontainable love responded to unfathomable *Love* in a beautiful display.

Whether we raise hands high to Holy, hand over our "to-do" lists, or take our pasts to the feet of Jesus, He sees our hearts. He's honored with hearts bowed low in humble worship. Presenting ourselves and every aspect of our lives to Him is a sweet smelling aroma.

Questions

1. What is your story?

2. In Romans 1:16, what did Paul say about telling others about Jesus? Have you told your story of how Jesus has changed your life? Start preparing yourself to share by writing at least some key words of your story. Practice telling it in 5 minutes or less.

3. Read Luke 7:47. What does this verse mean to you? Who do you relate with more in this story, the pharisee or the woman at Jesus' feet?

4. Read John 5:21-23, 2 Timothy 4:8, and James 4:12. What do these verses say about judging? Have you ever judged or misunderstood another Christian with zeal? As a Christian, have

you noticed yourself having little patience with people who may not look, act, or worship like you?

5. Have you been misunderstood? How did it make you feel?

6. Would you agree that worship is more than music? List some other ways you can worship God with your life?

7. What is the most important aspect of worship to you? What draws you personally closest to God? (For example, nature, worship in song, praising God for who He is through prayer, reading the Word, a great message from the Word, or ministering to others?)

For soaking, listen to:

Kari Jobe. "Revelation Song" *Kari Jobe*

Nine

One Flesh

"I am my beloved's, And my beloved is mine."
~ Song of Solomon 6:3

A friend asked if David and I were doing anything special for our wedding anniversary. We normally try to get away or at least have a date night. Turns out this year we didn't have anything planned. There was a time when having no special plans would have highly disappointed me. This time I responded in a way that even surprised me. I said, "You know, the longer I'm married the less I need *things*. Yes it would be nice to do something special, but honestly my husband is the greatest anniversary present. I'm just happy to have him. I'm in love with him more every day, and he *is* the gift. I don't need any-*thing*."

David and I don't have this marriage thing perfected but we've been happily married for eighteen years, with a few (aheem) exceptional moments. After reading the first chapter of this book you can understand the miracle in that statement! God is still saving and restoring hopeless marriages, including ours when we had lost hope. My husband and I still have heated come-to-Jesus meetings on occasion, but we work through disagreements better now than fifteen years ago. Marriage is not always easy. But on good days it's a walk in the park with the one you love and a bed of roses to go with it.

Letting Jesus be central to our marriage is the most important lesson we've learned in all of our years together. He honors us making Him the priority of our lives. Period. In everything. Consult God first by praying together and letting Holy Spirit lead. Pray! The saying goes, "A family that prays together stays together." There's a lot of truth to that statement. I've never seen genuine prayer between two people cause an argument, but I *have* seen it dissolve arguments. With that said, pray often *for and with* one another. Jesus said,

> *Again, truly I tell you that if two of you on earth agree about anything they ask for, it will be done for them by my Father in heaven (Matthew 18:19).*

Imagine how powerful for two people who have come together through the covenant promise of marriage to agree in prayer! Often people will say, "Well, my husband and I pray, we just don't pray together." It might feel a little awkward at first, but I encourage you to try it. Nothing says intimacy like pouring your heart out to God with your spouse listening in and agreeing. All marriages are different, and people are in different places in their journey with God. But God delights when we seek and follow Him in all matters of business *and* pleasure.

I'll admit as a young woman I was extremely stubborn. I was determined that it may not be such a great idea for me to ever get married. I knew several couples who had gotten married too young, had children too early, and argued a lot. None of these appealed to me. The "good" marriages I observed who stuck it out for years didn't seem all that blissfully happy. I couldn't imagine signing up to be unhappy for the rest of my life. I couldn't wrap my mind around the whole idea of answering to a man. Not a chance! I remember stating with boldness, "I'm never getting married. No way! That whole having to submit thing is nuts, crazy if you ask me!" Of course God had a different plan. I've painted a picture for you of my strong-willed nature which is still strong but exceptionally more under control. Underneath my attitude I was a girl who desperately wanted what God wanted for her.

I met David during one of his annual trips to visit his family in North Carolina. I was in college and for the first time in my life "no way" changed to "hmmm... maybe." Three years later I married him and followed him to California. *Many are the plans of a man's (or woman's) heart , but it's God's purpose that prevails (Proverbs 19:21, emphasis mine)*, and I was proof. God's ways and plans were bigger and better than mine, and they prevailed for sure.

THE "S" WORD

The first years of our marriage were good but could've been so much easier. I was full of myself, prideful and self-centered. Looking back there were several contributing factors to my difficult behavior: a new state, new home, new job, new friends, new family (some who had not accepted me), new church, new, new, new. All of this newness equaled stress. I was insecure, emotional, demanding, controlling, and immature to say the least. Oh I had my list of good qualities but my nagging made for an interesting start. At the root of it was control. There were so many things in my life that felt out of my control, I tried to compensate by controlling my husband. I was so afraid of becoming his doormat, I turned him into mine without realizing it.

I wanted what God wanted for me. Sure, I wanted to live a life pleasing to Him, but in my marriage I conveniently left out the parts about love and respect. Oh I loved to the best of my ability. Truth is, I really didn't understand love so loving selflessly was tough. *Love keeps no record of wrongs.* I constantly brought up the past and resurrected every mistake my husband had ever made. Respect is esteeming others above ourselves. I showed him little respect. I was in no way surrendered to God in the area of honoring and submitting to my husband. My words and strong will didn't reflect the love of Jesus. Praise God I married a patient man who did exemplify Christ in the way He loved me in return.

Submitting is still a challenge on some days and I don't claim to have it all figured out, but God's taught me that my marriage is a picture of my relationship with Jesus. God created earthly love, pursuit, marriage, and sex to exemplify the love relationship between He and His bride. As part of the Bride, or the Church, Jesus is our spiritual Husband. He's the Bridegroom. It finally occurred to me, if what I have with my husband is supposed to demonstrate what I have with Jesus, how can I possibly honor God without honoring my husband? How can I say that I love Jesus and raise my hands in praise in church then go home and dishonor my earthly husband. Respecting my husband goes hand in hand with loving God with all my heart.

> *See then that you walk circumspectly, not as fools but as wise, redeeming the time, because the days are evil. Therefore do not be unwise, but understand what the will of the Lord is. /giving thanks always for all things to God the Father in the name of our Lord Jesus Christ, submitting to one another in the fear of God (Ephesians 5:15-17, 20-21).*

My husband is to be the head of the home as Christ is the head of the church. In the past I struggled with letting him be the head of our home. Paul clearly points out the will of God is to stay away from evil, give thanks for all things, and submit to *one another* out of respect for God. This helps me. This means submitting is for *all people,* a yielding to one another in every direction. Yes verse 22 clearly indicates wives are to submit to their husbands, but the verses before it are often overlooked. Submitting to *one another i*s the will of God. This means we should never be a doormat for anyone.

> *Wives, submit to your own husbands, as to the Lord. For the husband is head of the wife, as also Christ is head of the church; and He is the Savior of the body. Therefore, just as the church is subject to Christ, so let the wives be to their own husbands in everything.*
>
> *Husbands, love your wives, just as Christ also loved the church and gave Himself for her, that He might sanctify and cleanse her with the washing of water by the word, that He might present her to Himself a glorious church, not having spot or wrinkle or any such thing, but that she should be holy and without blemish. So husbands ought to love their own wives as their own bodies; he who loves his wife loves himself (Ephesians 5: 22-28).*

He tells *men to love their wives as Christ loved the church and gave Himself up for her.* This means he should love his wife so relentlessly and sacrificially he would die for her. He should love her as much as He loves his own body, with unconditional grace and favor. I know some men who *really* love their own bodies. Admiring themselves, they highly value their time at the gym. They strut and model in front of the mirror with passion. If these men love and honor their wives, investing in them with the care they have for their own bodies, their wives should be abundantly blessed. If some of the single men who come to mind ever get married and live by this principle, they'll make wonderful husbands!

When our men love us as described in these verses, we can't help but love in return. We're smitten. We want to do whatever they want. We'll go out of our way to make their favorite meal, play their favorite song, or ask to hear about their day. When we're still pursued by our husbands several years into marriage, we'll overlook how tired we are to carve out time for most anything, including sex. In the same way we love Jesus because He first loved us, so shouldn't we also love our husbands simply because they love us?

I'VE GOT THE POWER

God has helped me discover the privilege of being a woman. What we have is beautiful and powerful, but this power should never be misused as manipulation. If you don't believe me, read the story of Adam and Eve or Samson and Delilah. A woman's power, if used responsibly, can motivate her man to be all he was created to be and more. Several years ago, I saw a movie where the man--speaking to his woman--said: "You make me a better man." We have the capacity for this. To make our men even better than they already are. Hopefully our men do the same for us, make us better versions of ourselves.

1. **Power to release control.**

It's no wonder men aren't the spiritual leaders of the average Christian home. We're afraid to allow them to be. We can't seem to let go. If we do encourage them to lead it's often with nagging. Proverbs says, *"A quarrelsome wife is like a constant dripping,"* annoying! Instead of nagging choose words that encourage and inspire. I often say our words are like bras, they should never be used as sling shots. They were meant to lift and enhance. When we trust God and release control, we empower our husbands to be the men God designed them to be: the head of the home, lover, provider, and protector.

2. **Power to meet his needs.**

My husband loves me selflessly. He's forgiven me. He goes out of his way to serve and provide. He meets my emotional needs by listening and caring. With humility and gentleness, he reminds me to say no when I want to say yes. He keeps me balanced. A provider to our family and protector, he seriously loves like Jesus.

Guess what this does for me? It causes me to want to do whatever he wants within reason. I'm willing to submit, yield, serve and love him, not because I have to but because I really want to. He treats me like a queen, and in return I want him to feel like a king. I take care of his needs. It's a two way street. We both selflessly give one hundred percent to the relationship, and it works!

Eve was created to be Adam's helper, his help-meet. Most of us would think nothing of helping an elderly person cross the street or serving at the nearest soup kitchen. Building our children up and serving them in every way is no problem for us. So why then do we find it so difficult to serve and love our men selflessly? It's sad when we are more kind to strangers than we are to our God-given life partners. We aren't living the life God created for us as women if we aren't helping meet the needs of our husbands, whatever they may be.

My husband recently shared a story he heard. In a scientific study of fruit flies, male fruit flies are extremely aggressive. (I hate fruit flies with a passion, so the fact that I'm writing about them is almost comical.) The pheromones produced by the female have a calming effect on the aggressive males. Their calmer behavior had nothing to do with sex, though that was normally a result of them being in close proximity for any length of time. The study proved, even without sex the males mellowed in the presence of the females. Even nasty, annoying fruit flies were created specifically for the females to help meet the needs of their male counterpart.

Meeting our husband in the bedroom is one of the more fun ways we can meet his needs. Some women would disagree. For a multitude of reasons, we are uncomfortable talking about it. Because the world has twisted it into something sinful and ugly, we shy away from admitting that we enjoy it. We tend to forget that God created it beautifully to be shared between a man and woman within marriage. With that said, our conversations about sex outside of marriage should be pure and tasteful, leaving the details in the bedroom.

I recently saw a movie where the couple was in counseling, and the husband admitted his sexual fantasy was to have a threesome. This is the sad reality of our culture, where married men and women dream of having sex with more than one partner.

I'd like to offer up the idea that sex in marriage can be fantasy-like without a third party. If you insist on the necessity of a third party to spice things up, that third party should be God Himself. Wait a minute, don't be offended. Hear me out! I mean if we put God at the center of all we do, He'll make it great whatever it is--including sex! God created the sexual relationship between a man and woman to be one of the most enjoyable aspects of marriage. Sexual intimacy is literally as close as we ever get to another person, physically. It's becoming one flesh as Jesus suggested,

> *And He answered and said to them, "Have you not read that He who made them at the beginning 'made them male and female,' and said, 'For this reason a man shall leave his father and mother and be joined to his wife, and the two shall become one flesh?' So then, they are no longer*

two but one flesh. Therefore what God has joined together, let not man separate " (Matthew 19:4-6).

Becoming *one flesh* is designed to be a pleasant experience, not something to be dreaded. God really does want us to enjoy it. Great sex starts long before we hit the sheets. It starts with words, acts of service, emotions, and meaningful touch before the bedroom. Taking the time to simply touch one another often, then being willing to explore to figure out what works and what doesn't, contributes to making it great.

Now the body is not for sexual immorality but for the Lord, and the Lord for the body./ do you not know that your body is the temple of the Holy Spirit who is in you, whom you have from God, and you are not your own? For you were bought at a price; therefore glorify God in your body and in your spirit, which are God's (1 Corinthians 6:13b, 20).

Coming together as one in marriage is glorifying to God. He knew who our spouse would be before we did, and He created our bodies to fit perfectly together. How lovely is that? Your body was made for your husband's. Not only were we fearfully and wonderfully made, so was our spouse fearfully and wonderfully for us! As I thought about this, I couldn't help but think through a few of the obstacles to great sex in marriage.

-Need for communication. Commonly women feel their husbands want *sex* but don't necessarily want *them.* This is a problem. If this is how you feel, please communicate. Most men are not mind readers. More than likely this is not how he feels at all. This is probably your perception of how he feels. Men are visual and physical in the way they feel and give love. Because we're more verbal, women tend to need affirmation. We need to know we've been noticed, admired, and loved simply for who we are.

-*Never quite satisfied.* Most women need time and have to be warmed up. Men are ready before they even get to the first kiss. For a lot of women this is a huge problem. Their man isn't willing to wait. Guys, your waiting is often key to our satisfaction and well worth it-- or so I've been told. Don't rush.

-*Lack of emotional and spiritual intimacy.* Women are communicators, so being heard and understood on an emotional level helps us connect physically. Inviting Holy Spirit into the process seems crazy, but I encourage you to try it. I'm not implying we should invite God to have sex with us. I'm just saying God created sex, so it's silly to think He couldn't answer prayers to make it more wonderful than anything we've ever experienced. We have God's favor and approval to freely enjoy sex with our spouse. When we make our relationship with Him a priority as a couple, then every other aspect of our relationship will begin to grow, including sexual enjoyment.

-*Guilt over the past.* Condemnation from past decisions or past abuse can cause major problems in marital intimacy. *There is no condemnation for those who are in Christ (Romans 8:1).* If the decision was yours and you've repented and asked for forgiveness, then allow Jesus to forgive. When He forgives He remembers it no more. When you think about that sin, praise Jesus for forgiving and forgetting.

If it was abuse, talk to God and let Him begin healing it so you can be free to move forward. Ask Him to help you forgive your abuser. Lack of healing can ruin intimacy with your spouse and could potentially ruin your marriage.

-*Body Image.* In a world saturated with porn addictions and fantasies of threesomes, it's no wonder so many women feel insecure when they look in the mirror. No matter our size, color, or shape, God created all women beautifully. You are no fantasy--you are the real deal! Be confident in that! Understand that you are the only one given permission by God to sexually please your husband. Remember he chose you to marry, not someone else. Be confident that you are loved by God *and* your husband.

3. Power to communicate effectively and regularly.

Think and pray before you speak. Always make solid communication a priority. Remember nothing should ever have to be hidden from your spouse, so be transparent. Part of being intimate is allowing the other person to see into you and know you in the deepest places. It's much deeper than sex, it's allowing them to see into your soul. If you can't have this first with God and then with your spouse, you shouldn't have it with anyone. Being open and honest is vital to every healthy marriage.

Affirm often. Most people respond positively to affirmation. When we affirm we tell the person that they have value. Everyone likes to feel appreciated. Valuing our spouses demonstrates respect which is something that causes them to soar, and typically they begin returning the favor. Purposefully think of ways to encourage. Whatever you do, don't provoke! For some reason we have a few days out of each month (aka PMS) when hormones cause us to want to pick a fight or kill something. My advice--don't talk that week! If something ills you, keep it to yourself. There's a good chance you're being irrational. After that week if it still bothers you, prayerfully bring it up. We all remember the childhood saying, "If you can't say anything nice, don't say anything at all." Be POSITIVE!

4. Power to delight.

I see him staring at me from across the room and I love it, especially when he doesn't know I've noticed. My man is adamant that the only problem he has with lust is his lust for his wife. Guys, your woman wants the assurance you're not addicted to porn, you're just addicted to her! If you want to get a response from her, let her know you still find her sexy and beautiful. Don't just tell her, show her. Pursue her. Admire her from across the room. Delight in her!

Remember why you got married in the first place. What was your vision for marriage? What were your spouse's ideas? Are you carrying them out? Create ways to carry out your mission together. What drew you to them? What did you love most? Cling to those things. Get creative to keep those things alive in your marriage. For example if you adored the way he made you laugh, do something to spark the silliness in him. Remind him of how much you love his sense of humor. Remind him of some of the reasons why you fell in love with him. Write these things down in your journal as reminders to yourself.

Think of ways to make coming home exciting and inviting for your man and not something he dreads. If you can, have dinner started. Hug, take his hand, or greet him with a kiss. Give him a quick shoulder rub if this is something he enjoys. Make flirting a priority. My husband and I don't wait for special occasions to date. We have candle-lit date nights at home, if our children are with grandparents. We're playful in the kitchen, office or wherever. We allow our children to see us loving on one another. It's healthy for them to witness hugs, kisses, and little flirtatious comments.

Most of our children have heard us arguing, which is hopefully rare. If they hear our occasional spats, they should also see us making up. It's good for them to know mama and daddy are in love. It demonstrates healthiness and balance in marriage.

Because men are generally visual, they enjoy coming home to us put together. Walking in from work to us still wearing our flannel pajama pants and flip flops isn't attractive to most men. It's speaks loudly that we don't care or that we've lost interest in caring. How hard is it to put on something nice every now and then?

An even more special gesture is when we take the time to wear something sexy to bed. Honestly, it's not going to be on that long anyway, so what's the big deal? It's like wrapping a gift. This doesn't have to be difficult. Put yourself in a pretty package and present it. Most men really appreciate us caring enough to do this. We don't have to be a size two to be sexy. Bodies change with time. Inevitably none of us look the way we did when we were sixteen, not even the ones who spend lots of time trying. No amount of money or surgery can buy our youth. Loving ourselves just the way we are, extra wrinkles and pounds and all, is sexy. Confidence is pretty and contagious.

We can help-meet our husband's needs from the kitchen to the bedroom. When we decide to do this, his response to us can't help but be positive. I realize there are exceptions, so don't allow yourself to be mistreated. You're worth more than that. But when we love deeply, we're changed deep. We worry about being liberated, powerful and modern women of this millennium. Trust me, it's most liberating to give way to a little fun and love him reckless.

ALL MY SINGLE LADIES

All my single ladies--throw your hands up! I remember being single and waiting for my love. At night while lying in my bed as a teenage girl I would pray for my future husband and children. In your own wait enjoy life. Press on and press in to *Love*. Do all the things you'll wish you could do once you're married with children, like traveling and using the toilet without an audience.

Love will try to awaken prematurely. Creating boundaries and deciding what's negotiable and what isn't ahead of time will make it easier to measure character and avoid disaster. If this man honors your boundaries, then he'll respect you in other areas. Be sure he meets God's standards. Be on guard to give yourself to the one God has chosen for you, which may or may not be the first one who comes along.

> *I charge you, O daughters of Jerusalem, Do not stir up nor awaken love Until it pleases (Song of Solomon 8:4).*

Knowing the possibility of sexual temptation and sexually transmitted diseases, God says *not to stir up love* prematurely. He says to *keep the marriage bed pure.* One way to do this is to avoid sex before marriage. Doing so will help prevent insecurities related to being compared to another woman, or comparing your man to some other man. God wants to protect you in every way--before and after marriage.

Purity is not just about virginity, and just because someone is a virgin does not mean they're pure. Purity is a matter of the mind, eyes and heart, as well as how you treat your body. Trying people on for size is not necessary to know which person is a fit for marriage, sexually or in any other way. If sex is a requirement to date them, you don't need them. Sex can confuse, causing you to think you're in love when you're really in lust. Feeling guilty that you've prematurely given yourself away can cause you to settle for the wrong person for life. Simply put, saving yourself sexually will save you a lot of heartache. God has your future spouse selected already. The one He's handpicked for you is a perfect fit in every way, by Divine design. Wait on Him. Pursue *Love* first, then He'll show you who He's chosen to be your earthly love.

Purity comes from God. If you feel like you've blown it in the purity department, it doesn't mean you can never be pure again.

Ask God to forgive you and move forward. Don't return to it and in His eyes you are as pure as if it never happened. That's not to say premarital sex won't come with some consequences. It very well may. That is to say God will forgive and forget. He doesn't expect you to live in guilt for the rest of your life. You are His treasure. He loves you no matter what. Believe it, embrace it and live like it! You are made clean and pure in His sight!

Beauty is not defined by physical appearance, though it's totally okay to dress cute and feel good about the way you look. Godly character makes you beautiful. Instead of worrying about whether you're wearing designer clothes, worry about whether you're dressed in the ultimate Designer's clothes…love, purity, honesty, kindness, joy, peace, patience, goodness, faithfulness, gentleness, and self-control. God's duds are so much better than the world's.

Attention can't substitute true love. Wearing a shirt with "I'm Sexy and I Know It" written across the front is *not* sexy! This screams insecurity and an unhealthy need for attention. Dressing with class and leaving room for the imagination *is* sexy. Cover yourself. They're called privates for a reason, so keep them that way! Stringy tops, cleavage hanging out, and unzipped short shorts will get attention, but I can promise it will be the wrong kind. Don't give it away right away. Save it for your future husband.

Bad company corrupts good character, so choose your friends wisely and ask God to guide you in the process. When you go on a date, even if the other person pays, you owe them nothing but a "thank you" and a "good night." With every decision there's a consequence. Think first and make wise choices.

When dating, be yourself! Don't pretend to be someone you're not to impress. And on the flip side, don't try to change the other person into who you want them to be. When something about the person bothers you while you're dating, it will only get worse when you marry. Don't think marriage will fix it. Find someone with similar interests and values, or someone who will appreciate and respect yours. Dating a person who hates what you love or loves what you hate can be terribly frustrating. Dating is for eventual marriage. God wants you to have a marriage partner who will either join you in His calling for your life, or support and enhance it. And remember to laugh. If you argue a lot, there's a good chance you shouldn't be together.

Trust is a vital part of any relationship. If you can't trust them, don't marry them.

Whether married or single, Jesus is our Husband. *Arouse and awaken* to His love. He's in pursuit of us every single day and shows us the real meaning of intimacy. We *can* trust Him! The longer we're *one* with *Love,* the less we need things. With Him we find ourselves doing and getting unexpected, sweet gifts all the time. In love with Him more every day, He *is* the gift. We don't need any-*thing*. We just need Him.

Questions

1. Read: Ephesians 5:15-33 and Genesis 2:18-25. What have your feelings been about submitting to your husband? After reading the full context of these verses, what are your feelings?

2. How are you doing with showing your husband love through submission and being his help-meet? In what ways could you improve?

3. Read: 1 Corinthians 13. List some qualities of love. How are you doing loving the way love is described in these verses?

4. If you are single, are you dating? What nonnegotiable standards do you have for your future spouse? Is Jesus at the center of your relationship? In what ways are you keeping God a priority as a couple? Do you have the same vision for marriage?

5. How are you doing with creating clear boundaries physically? Is this person God's choice for you for marriage? Does he treat you with the respect and love of Jesus? Do you treat him with the respect and love of Jesus? List some ways you could improve.

While you wait for Mr. Right, ask God to satisfy your every desire. Ask Him to arouse and awaken love in His timing. Trust Him to give you the contentment you need while you wait.

For soaking, listen to:

Cory Asbury. "Where I Belong" *Let Me See Your Eyes*

His-Story

"When we submit our lives to what we read in Scripture, we find that we are being led not to see God in our stories but to see our stories in God's. God is the larger context and plot in which our stories find themselves." ~ Eugene Peterson

There's nothing like a sharp toy under bare feet in the dark to bring a grown woman to her knees. I remember like it was yesterday stepping on pointed objects in the night. He'd make things, building something from nothing. He would say, "Hey mom, look at this! What do you think?" In free time he stacked one on top of the other. Lego's covered the floor.

She would ask, "Mom, do you have a glue gun? Could you help me glue this rhinestone onto my new hair bow?" It was endless what their little minds could imagine!

God's creativity is beyond our thinking. The world He merely spoke into existence is so complex that some of the most brilliant men to ever live deny that God created it. They can't wrap their minds around it so they seek to explain it away. As they have attempted to prove the "big bang theory," scientists have discovered multiple galaxies. Despite their pursuit to disprove Creationism, the findings consistently point to a Creator-God who continues to leave us in awe of His creation. Each galaxy was created with order and intention, a perfect and masterful work of art.

A. W. Tozer wrote,

> "The Word of God is quick and powerful. In the beginning He
> spoke to nothing, and it became something. Chaos heard it and
> became order, darkness heard it and became light."

It all started in the beginning. He *is* the beginning! His story is of goodness,
faithfulness and life-changing love--our Creator and His creation, hand in
hand. On the sixth day God said,

> *Let us make man in Our image, according to Our likeness, let*
> *them have dominion... over all the earth/ And the Lord God*
> *formed man of the dust of the ground, and breathed into his*
> *nostrils the breath of life; and man became a living being*
> *(Genesis 1:26; 2:7).*

Us implies the presence of more than one person: Father, Son and Holy
Spirit. Jim Reimann wrote,

> "Though the word trinity is not in the Bible, it is biblical. A
> helpful way to consider the three persons of the one God is to
> think of the Father as the 'Will of God,' the Son as the 'Word of
> God,' and the Spirit as the 'Power of God.'"

Though Jesus' name is not spelled out in Genesis, His presence is
inferred. The Son was with the Father and Holy Spirit in the beginning,
creating. Jesus, the Word who became flesh and dwelt among us, was
there speaking worlds into existence and breathing life into the nostrils
of humanity. Intimacy at it's finest.

> *In the beginning was the Word, and the Word was with God,*
> *and the Word was God. He was in the beginning with God.*

All things were made through Him, and without Him nothing was made that was made (John 1:1-3).

At age 3 my son asked, "If God created everything, then who created God Mama? Was He all alone? Who was His Mama?"

I replied, "That's a good question honey. God doesn't have a mama. He's always been and always will be. That's why one of His names is the Ancient of Days. We'll have to ask Him all about it when we see Him."

"When will we see Him?" he asked. I marveled at his curious mind.

"When we die and go to heaven," I replied. Satisfied, he returned to playing.

It's difficult to explain to a 3-year old that we have daily access to God, who transcends time and space exceeding universes unseen.

In the beginning He created the heavens and the earth (Genesis 1:1).

By the word of the Lord were the heavens made, and all the host of them by the breath of His mouth (Psalm 33:6).

Our Creator-God who made stars to sing and brushes pink and golden sunsets across the canvas of the sky, breathes life through His Word into human hearts. The Word of God is His story. Alive, it guides us to a deeper understanding of Him. It makes sense, because He *is* the Word. His Word is the written account of creation, our sin, His love for us and His plan for redeeming and reconciling us back to Himself through Jesus.

In the Garden of Eden, God created humans to have relationship with Him and worship Him. Eve's wandering curiosity resulted in sin, and His story took a different turn. Or did it? Adam and Eve's sin did not surprise God. He knew humanity's demise ahead of time and planned accordingly. He recognized our need for a Savior. He knew many would doubt and reject Him, but out of His great love for humanity He provided a way to forgiveness. And through faith in Him, we have hope. Jesus has given each of us the opportunity to have soul-life, the kind that resurrects us out of our old habits and mindsets making us new creations in Him.

Whether we will believe is a decision we all have to make. In John 18 moments before Jesus was crucified, onlookers observed. Peter cut the high priest's servant's ear off with his sword and Jesus healed him. To have compassion to heal one of the men who would momentarily carry Him to His death is almost unimaginable, yet His love for mankind superseded everything else. He performed a miracle before their eyes. The officers from the chief priests and Pharisees fell to their knees when Jesus answered, *"I am He."*

They knew who He was. They witnessed it firsthand, yet their hearts were hardened with evil. Their pride persisted and carried Him to the cross. Pride keeps us from giving in and submitting to anyone *other* than ourselves. It keeps us from giving in to belief. When Jesus returns every knee will bow before Him.

> *God also has highly exalted Him and given Him the name which is above every name, that at the name of Jesus every knee should bow, of those in heaven, and of those on earth, and of those under the earth, and that every tongue should confess that Jesus Christ is Lord, to the glory of God the Father (Philippians 2:9-11).*

OUR STORY

With creation, this Divine occupation of fashioning something from dirt, we see the miracle of life. Two cells, a sperm and an egg marry to become one. Our identity is established, and the blueprint for our make-up is in place. Cells duplicate, DNA formulas are magnificently and perfectly put in place. Uniquely designed, no two people have the same fingerprints. Just as our world and the worlds around us were created deliberately, so was every muscle, bone, organ, and joint in the human body. Orderly and miraculous, the intricacies of creation are displayed in humanity. In pregnancy when a woman feels her baby move inside like butterfly kisses, the Artist's fingertips are brushing the canvas of an individual. God-breath breathes and warm life springs up. Our story is really His.

Crying over what I thought God had promised, I frequently asked my husband, "Do you think we'll ever have children?" After waiting and praying for what seemed like an eternity, God remembered. He moved, faithful to His promise. Hunter was my first child. Had his birth been in my timing rather than God's, he wouldn't be the same boy. Genetic combinations would've been different. God knew what He was doing when He fashioned my son, and as always His timing was perfect. God had my baby's days ordained and numbered, like mine and yours, from before the beginning of time.

She wept and waited and He held her. God remembered Hannah and gave her a son. She felt her baby move inside, and in return for His remembrance and answered prayer she gave him back to God. After all, Samuel was already His long before his conception. *"Samuel grew in stature and in favor with the Lord and with men"* (1 Samuel 2:26). He played a significant role in God's Story. Samuel listened and followed God to anoint young David as King over Israel. Through David's lineage, Jesus was born. Hannah had no idea her deepest desire to have a baby, her prayers and waiting, even her willingness and obedience to give him back, was all part of God's story.

There's power and purpose in our stories. Each day we write another page with words, pictures, actions, movement, breath, accomplishment and failure. They not only heal us as we share them but they open others up to healing. God knows our stories before we know them ourselves. They fit perfectly into His plan layer upon layer. He knew before the beginning of time the very day and exact millisecond of our birth, how many days we would spend on earth, and what we would spend them doing.

> *For we are His workmanship, created in Christ Jesus for good works, which God prepared beforehand that we should walk in them (Ephesians 2:10).*

GOD'S VISION

We don't always see what God sees. Feelings cloud our vision. With difficulty fathoming why our all-sufficient God would want to use us, we see ourselves as ordinary but He sees His masterpiece. We have a guaranteed purpose because He doesn't make mistakes.

Several years ago God gave me a desire to write weekly devotions for the church I attended. Since it's a church with several thousand in attendance, I was not confident to pursue what I knew God was telling me to do. In passing I asked one of my friends on staff what the requirements were for writing. She told me there were only a handful of people on the devotions team. It seemed exclusive, but she gave me a contact name if I had more questions. I never pursued it.

A year or so passed. After a conversation with my brother (a phenomenal writer) Holy Spirit prompted and I knew I had to start writing somewhere. I felt strongly it was to be more than private journaling which I had always done. My brother mentioned starting a blog. Visiting his blog a few times summed up my exposure to the blog world. I decided to give it a try thinking it would leave a legacy:

something for my children and grandchildren to enjoy one day. When I first started my blog posts were made public for other bloggers who might happen upon them, but I never intentionally shared. Finding my blog required searching.

After posting fairly consistently for a few months, one of the devotion's team leaders from my church somehow found my blog. Taking the time to comment, she encouraged me to pray about being on the writing team. I saw God clearly through that chain of events and knew His answer right away. Even through my lack of confidence, He saw and knew what I needed. He had birthed the idea of being on that team in my heart. It was His dream that I write. As only He could, He faithfully provided to fulfill His own will and purpose in my life. He knew what faithfulness in writing would one day lead to. He saw the overall plan.

> *For as the heavens are higher than the earth, So are My ways higher than your ways, And My thoughts than your thoughts (Isaiah 55:9).*

The big picture is in God's view. He's the guy standing on top of the building watching the parade. He can see the beginning, the end, and everything in between. He already knows it all which makes His vision for our lives a lot clearer than our own. To know His vision for us we have to learn to see Him with our hearts and not our literal eyes. We have to ask Him to *enlighten the eyes of our hearts.*

Pray, "Lord help me to know You and Your will for my life by opening my spiritual eyes and ears to see and hear You today. Make Your Word come alive in my life. Show Yourself to me." He will reveal Himself.

When we get quiet before God with His Word, then comes, as A. W. Tozer wrote,

> "the happy moment when the Spirit begins to illuminate the Scriptures, and that which had been only a sound, or at best a voice, now becomes an intelligible word, warm and intimate and clear as the word of a dear friend. Then will come life and light, and best of all, ability to see and rest in and embrace Jesus Christ as Saviour and Lord and All" (*The Pursuit of God*).

Listen closely and let Him lead. Whatever He's asking of you He will enable you to do, if you're willing to journey with Him. When we get ahead or off course, the road becomes more challenging. Doing great things for God takes some effort and willingness to move. Writing wasn't always easy. When the writing team leader welcomed me to the team, her words were, "It'll make you a better writer." She was right. There were times writing one paragraph took hours. The devotion for the day had to be summed up in a few words. This took effort. With dedication, preparing, and the faithful prayers of others, serving on that team pushed me to be better. God used that season in my life to prepare me for even more. I'm a strong communicator and writing was one of the tools He wanted me to use to do that.

God has given each of us abilities, spiritual gifts, and gifts of the Spirit that are unique to our personalities. He wants us to discover our abilities, uncover our gifts, and walk in them. (There are many great resources: books, websites, and classes for discovering spiritual gifts.) Actively living out our passions and the plans God has for us, we find the most joy and make the biggest impact. He will take our little bit and turn it into greatness when we're willing to say yes.

Throughout history God raised up the humble and gave strength to the weary. He took the yeses of ordinary people and changed history. David was a young shepherd boy but God raised Him up to become king over Israel. Very little is known about Joel except God gave Him prophetic vision for the Church. He wasn't famous but God entrusted him with the important task of speaking His words to His people. Amos, a mere herdsman, was used to prophesy and preach. Daniel was a teenage boy sent away from his home and family to work in another country. As God would have it he moved up in ranks under the king of that foreign territory, and God used him to interpret important dreams for the king.

Risking her life for her people, Esther was chosen. Her life's purpose was *"for such a time as this,"* to become queen and save Israel. God used her because she chose to say yes to Him. She was given much and much was required of her position. Before risking her life to approach the king on their behalf, Esther sent a message asking the Jews to fast and pray alongside her for three days. The king's favor was extended, her people were saved, and she fulfilled her destiny and purpose as queen.

You've been chosen for something special in this life that only you can do! Age doesn't matter, appearance makes no difference, even education is of no huge significance. You are God's child. That's enough. Designed specifically for a purpose, you have a story and an ability for such a time as this. Esther's yes changed generations. We have no idea (but God does) how our yes could significantly bend history.

Each of these heroes were ordinary people who worshipped God by going when He said go. They caught the vision God had for them. They saw themselves as small and God as big. They trusted in the sovereignty of God. Experiencing His faithfulness fully, they stepped out. This uncontainable God with whom they were intimately acquainted--Who is *"far above all principality and power and might and dominion, and every name that is named, not only in this age but also in that which is to come" (Ephesians 1:21)*--reached into their insignificant corners of the world and raised them up.

If we ask, He will share the vision He has for our lives and how we fit into His story. As members of His body, we are part of the grander story. Every person belonging to God make up the Body of Christ, or the Church. I'm not referring to a building with four walls, I mean the Church collectively across the nations. We are the church, as we have Holy Spirit living inside us. We come together to make up the members of the Body. Each of us uniquely designed serve as different parts of the body. How beautiful is it when the body is in good health? When every person knows what God created them to do and they do it, the body doesn't survive it thrives!

Think about how difficult it would be for an eye to serve as a foot. It would be impossible, wouldn't it? It's a ridiculous thought. Often that's what happens in the church. People don't know what they were created for. They don't know their spiritual giftedness, so they find themselves functioning in the wrong capacity. There's nothing more frustrating. No orchestra needs fifty trumpets and one tiny flute. It takes balance and diversity to make a beautiful sound. We're all God's individual instruments, and He's given us each our own sound. Find your song and play it loud.

Rally around others to bring out their greatness. Learn to notice. Team building and pointing out people's strengths goes a long way to help them succeed. When my feet itch my hands do a great job scratching, and my eyes help guide my feet as they take steps. We can help one another by recognizing the needs and strengths of other the members of the body.

The body functions seamlessly when we live out the "one anothers" so often mentioned by Paul. Love one another. Encourage one another. Forgive one another. Pray for one another. Consider one another.

Gennie, my friend from Texas, was at a women's leadership conference in Charlotte a couple of years ago with her friend Meredith. Carole and I also attended the conference. Meredith and Carole met in a session on prayer, and they had the opportunity to pray together. Because they connected, she wanted Carole to meet Gennie. Shortly after their introduction Gennie introduced herself to me. Looking at my name tag she said, "Wait a minute. I saw your name in the prayer room. I prayed for you! Your name was under the same name of God as mine." Immediately we made a Holy Spirit connection.

Gennie and I exchanged information. Soon after the conference, I began to receive encouraging texts from her. We checked in every week or so. She and her family went through some unexpected difficulties in the weeks and months following. As God led she shared. I prayed and encouraged her in the midst of her trials. I saw God do the miraculous and was humbled to be a small part. Gennie is a huge cheerleader/ prayer warrior in my life. Along with so many others, she encouraged and prayed me through the writing of this book every step of the way.

After meeting for only five minutes face to face, it has been fascinating to watch Holy Spirit keep us connected. Through the timing and content of our texts, God has made Himself visible through our friendship. We weren't in close proximity, yet we championed one another. As different members of the Body, we were doing our individual parts to lift one another in special times of need. God ordained our meeting. We have stood in awe of Him, as our friendship has grown and as He's used it for His glory and kingdom plans. Soon I'll be speaking in Texas for a community-wide women's outreach event hosted by Gennie's church.

This will be our first time together since we met. God is amazing and His purposes prevail.

At the same conference in Charlotte a year later, I met Cynthia, Reiko and Lea from California. Cynthia and Reiko decided to come back the following January for a more intense version of the same conference. God had not confirmed that I should attend, nor did I have the finances. My friend Yvonne kept insisting if God wanted me there He would provide the money. Knowing Cynthia and Reiko would soon be coming in for the conference (only a few miles from my house), I wanted to see them while they were in Charlotte again. I connected with them to plan getting together for dinner while they were in town. Cynthia discovered last minute she couldn't attend the conference. Instead of taking the refund, she chose to bless me with her spot. I was overwhelmed by her generosity and the role she was willing to play in my life. She may never know her eternal investment until heaven, but her yes to God to bless me bent history. The Body *being* the Body is beautiful! God just needs us to do what He asks us to do *when* He asks us to do it.

Realize your strengths, passions, and calling probably will not be the same as others in the body. For example, people who are passionate about giving and serving don't always understand those with the gifts of teaching and exhorting. Polar opposites, the servers think the teachers should be serving more and vice versa. This is like the hands telling the mouth it needs to stop talking to do more dishes. Can you imagine trying to do dishes with your mouth? It would be impossible. The taste of soap would be disgusting. The point is, don't judge or expect everyone to be as passionate about your strengths as you are. Instead of becoming frustrated when other members of the body don't perform in the same capacity as you, encourage them in the ways they do serve.

If God says it, count on it. Whether you can see it or not, it's already in process. It will be in His timing, but He who calls is faithful. As the saying goes, "God doesn't call the equipped, He equips the called." We can not undo God's promises. If He promised, we can trust Him to do it.

Knowing God wanted to use me in women's ministry for many years, I wasn't sure how. My whole life He'd been preparing me for it. Surrounded by a mom, aunts, and grandmas who poured into me, I've unknowingly been on the receiving end of women's ministry for most of my years. Feeling completely inadequate to do any of what God was asking of me, I listened as He led and confirmed. God didn't tell me I would do women's ministry one day then put me on a platform to speak the next. It's been a process.

Everything in my life: nursing, worship, writing, teaching, leading, discipling, marriage, parenting, and friendship, has all been preparation for what is to come. I haven't arrived nor will I ever until I reach heaven, but I've lived and been shaped by successes and struggles. There's purpose in the wait. If you find yourself waiting, this season is preparing, healing, refining, and providing experiences necessary for your future.

Allow Holy Spirit to confirm and lead. Never get ahead of God. Strategies are great for messages, ministry, and marketing, but not necessary when God is given control. He's the greatest Strategist, Marketer, Inspirer, and Guide. Seek Him always.

Family is your first calling. Family was designed special so we could all be part of building God's Kingdom together. It's no accident that God gave you the parents, siblings, spouse, and/or children He did. Invest in your family and include them in what God's asking you to do if at all possible. Seasons change. This may be a time of being single, motherhood, being a grandparent, or taking care of aging parents. Remember those moments won't last forever. Try to enjoy them while you can. Every season has its perks.

Don't worry about what others are doing. Just because you wish you could do what someone else can doesn't necessarily mean God is calling you to it. Make sure you hear God clearly and follow Him. Where He wants you is the place of greatest joy and contentment. Normally His calling will line up with your passions, stories, and abilities. Don't make comparisons or try to be something you're not.

Give God the glory in every failure and success. If you ever think you've arrived, you've taken a wrong turn. You'll never fully arrive until you meet Jesus face to face. Be thankful and humbly worship God with your life.

You are living your God-given purpose right now. Don't think your calling is something to be obtained in the future. Realize you're in it. Living for and in Jesus moment by moment is the answer to His call. Each day ask, "What do You want from me today Lord? How can I live for you today? Bless me to be a blessing."

> *And we know that all things work together for good to those who love God, to those who are called according to His purpose (Romans 8:28).*

I love this promise. ALL things work together for good. When called according to God's purpose, every challenge we face and every success we celebrate is all for our good and His glory. He works it out. Part of His plan is His story unfolding with us in it!

My yes to God was saying yes to writing when no one read. It was consistently jotting down stories of seeing Him in everyday life. Many times I wanted to and could've quit, but I knew that wasn't what God wanted. He honors obedience. Remember how I had given up on writing this book and God showed me Nehemiah? God helped Nehemiah build that wall in record time. What should've taken years took fifty two days with God. Nehemiah prepared and prayed ahead, staying focused once he started. He had the favor of God with him and completed the task successfully.

Remember I felt there was no way I would write this book by Christmas, which was what I thought God had said? On the very day I decided to give up, He showed me the story of Nehemiah and had me count the days to Christmas. It was fifty two days exactly. As I write the last chapter, it is seven days until Christmas. I hope you see the miracle in that and stand in awe of God with me. Sure I've been writing for a few years, but God pulled ideas together for me. I was right, I *couldn't* write this book by Christmas, but He could! God does what He promises. He's a redeemer of time. NO-thing is too difficult for Him. He's Creator-God, who's still in the business of making things. He tells nothing to become something and it listens. How our story takes shape, depends on whether or not we listen and allow God to do the shaping.

Questions

1) Have you taken a spiritual gifts test? (If not, I encourage you to ask a church leader for the resources or find a test online.) If you have taken a test, what are your spiritual gifts or strengths? Are you utilizing the gifts God has given you to benefit the Body? How?

2) Are you allowing Jesus to have center-stage in your life?

If you knew today was one of your last, would you live differently? Will the pages of your life make a substantial difference in the grander story? What will you have accomplished by the end of your days?

3) What is God asking you to do? What do you believe God has chosen you for at "such a time as this?" Do you sense God nudging you to do something new? Are you willing to say yes? How could your yes bend history?

4) What are some of your concerns or fears about saying yes to God? Have you convinced yourself it's impossible to do what He wants?

5) Read Ephesians 3:20-21. What is the promise in these verses? Where is God's power at work?

6) Have you ever fallen into the comparison trap? Why is it dangerous to compare yourself to others?

For soaking, listen to:

Mary Kat Ehrenzeller. "Who Can Compare? (Live)" *EMERGING VOICES Jesus Culture Music*

Eleven

A Wedding

"And the Spirit and the bride say, 'Come!'" ~ Revelation 22:17a

Imagine being invited to the wedding of the Century. The invitation alone is frame-worthy. Your name hand-written in gold, trimmed with gold overlay, and dusted with diamond glitter, is at the center of the invitation. A dream come true, your airline tickets and hotel accommodations are inside. A hand-written letter from the bride informs of your future dress allowance and shopping spree to purchase the perfect gown for the occasion. You are an honored guest at the most famous wedding in history. In the front of the church you will be seated with the bride's family. At the reception there's a special seat with your name on it.

At a cost of $48 million, Prince Charles and Lady Diana's wedding in 1981 was the most expensive in history. With inflation, today that wedding would cost $110 million. Most of us who lived through the 80's still remember tuning in with 750 million others to watch this significant moment in history. Extravagant to say the least, Diana's wedding dress had a 25-foot train. Of the 27 wedding cakes, the main cake was 5 feet tall and took 14 weeks to prepare.

Such a special occasion, I remember preparing for months (actually years) to be ready for my wedding. All eyes were on me that day, so everything had to be in place. My nails were freshly and professionally done. My jewelry was perfect, and in place. A close friend styled my hair. My dress was a pure white, Italian silk sheath with vintage beading. Planned months ahead: every song, singer, and instrument was hand-picked. Every detail was considered including the traditional "something old, something new, something borrowed, and something blue." When the day finally came I was ready: physically, emotionally, and spiritually.

Weddings require preparation. I've known brides who have spent their whole lives dreaming of and planning their monumental day. Did you know there is going to be a wedding that will outshine the most glamorous weddings in history? The Bridegroom, Jesus is coming back to receive us, His bride. At this wedding we'll be more than an honored guest, we will be the ones dressed in white.

> *Let us be glad and rejoice and give Him glory, for the marriage of the Lamb has come, and His wife has made herself ready." And to her it was granted to be arrayed in fine linen, clean and bright, for the fine linen is the righteous acts of the saints (Revelation 19:7-8).*

In this revelation given to John by the angel of the Lord, *the marriage of the Lamb has come, and His wife has made herself ready.* She is *arrayed in fine linen, clean and bright.* She is pure without blemish. We are cleansed and righteous (made right before God), because of the cross of Jesus and the blood He shed. Her blemishes have been cleaned and covered by the blood of the Lamb. Jesus, the Lamb of God, is coming for His bride. The angel is saying this is what is to come. Since His return is imminent, are we ready? Is the bride ready for her Groom's coming?

Without going into a deep theological explanation of end times events, I want to be clear that Jesus *is* returning. Before Jesus' return to set up His kingdom on earth for a thousand years, several events have to occur: the rapture of the church, the rising of the anti-Christ, the tribulation, and the battle of Armageddon. There are different schools of thought regarding the order of these events. Regardless of their timing or order of occurrence, it's important to know they *will* happen. The question is are we ready and are we readying others?

In Matthew 25 Jesus used three parables to speak to His bride: the ten virgins, the servants and talents, the sheep and goats. He gave different scenarios to stress the importance of His bride being ready. Once He returns it will be too late. The ones who are not prepared at that point will simply not be invited in. The door will be closed. Now is the time for preparation: of our hearts, minds, and telling others. People: get ready!

Jesus wanted everyone to know so He gave three different examples to get the point clearly across. It's down right exciting to those who know without a doubt they are invited into the wedding but not so positive for those who are unsure.

In the first parable there were ten virgins. As was custom in Jewish culture, ten witnesses or virgins would be present for special occasions. Expecting a visit from the bridegroom the night before the wedding, the virgins would wait with lanterns to usher him into the house with light. Jesus referred to five of the virgins in this parable as wise and the other five as foolish. The wise virgins were prepared with lamps and extra oil as they waited for the Bridegroom.

> But while the bridegroom was delayed, they all slumbered and slept. "And at midnight a cry was heard: 'Behold, the bridegroom is coming; go out to meet him!' Then all those virgins arose and trimmed their lamps. And the foolish said to the wise, 'Give us some of your oil, for our lamps are

going out.' But the wise answered, saying, 'No, lest there should not be enough for us and you; but go rather to those who sell, and buy for yourselves.' And while they went to buy, the bridegroom came, and those who were ready went in with him to the wedding; and the door was shut.

Afterward the other virgins came also, saying, "Lord, Lord, open to us!" But he answered and said, "Assuredly, I say to you, I do not know you." Watch therefore, for you know neither the day nor the hour in which the Son of Man is coming (Matthew 25:5-13).

The ten virgins slept as they waited. For the five who were unprepared when the bridegroom returned, they were unable to enter in with him at the wedding. Are we using this time wisely? Are we prepared for His coming?

Jesus told the parable of the talents. The Master gave each of his servants differing amounts of talents (money), expecting them to invest wisely. One of the servants hid his talent. He was afraid to invest it. His master was so upset with his laziness, He threw him into the darkness. The thought of anyone being denied entrance through the door of heaven breaks my heart.

For the kingdom of heaven is like a man traveling to a far country, who called his own servants and delivered his goods to them. And to one he gave five talents, to another two, and to another one, to each according to his own ability; and immediately he went on a journey (Matthew 25:14-15).

Notice the talents in this story belonged to the Master, and He was disappointed that his servant didn't *know* Him well enough to know how He would want him to invest His talent. Everything we have belongs to God. Using what He's entrusted to us wisely, He wants us to make eternal investments.

Jesus wants us to know Him. We can't truly know Him if we're too busy or too afraid to spend time in His presence. Holy Spirit is how we really get to know Jesus. Holy Spirit is living inside us, but so many of us are afraid to experience Him intimately. Many church attenders have religion but not a real relationship with God. Some worship the pastor and not God. They follow the man, but not The Man! There's an epidemic of christians who are building their own kingdom under the name of building God's. God sees the hearts of men. Are we ready?

Jesus goes on in the third parable to describe the judgement of the nations.

> *When the Son of Man comes in His glory, and all the holy angels with Him, then He will sit on the throne of His glory. All the nations will be gathered before Him, and He will separate them one from another, as a shepherd divides his sheep from the goats (Matthew 25:31-32).*

At Jesus' second coming He will rule, reign, and judge all the nations and peoples of the earth. He will separate the people as a shepherd putting the sheep on His right and the goats on His left. The ones on His right will be invited into the Kingdom. Jesus explains in this parable,

> *Then the King will say to those on His right hand, 'Come, you blessed of My Father, inherit the kingdom prepared for you from the foundation of the world: for I was hungry and you gave Me food; I was thirsty and you gave Me drink; I was a stranger and you took Me in; I was naked*

> *and you clothed Me; I was sick and you visited Me; I was*
> *in prison and you came to Me" (Matthew 25:34-36).*

Unsure of what He meant they questioned, and He answered:

> *And the King will answer and say to them, 'Assuredly, I*
> *say to you, inasmuch as you did it to one of the least of*
> *these My brethren, you did it to Me" (Matthew 25:40).*

On the Great Day of the Lord a battle will be won and there will be a party going as Jesus' Kingdom is established here on earth! Our King of kings, Jesus, will judge the nations and all the saints of God will be celebrating with Him.

Meanwhile as the church of Jesus our calling is to take care of those in need. These three stories are all to motivate the bride. Jesus will return for His bride, and it may be sooner rather than later. Are we ready individually, and is the Church as a whole prepared to meet Jesus?

While we're waiting for Jesus' return revival is necessary to reach out, to bring healing, and to ready the world for His coming. Revival must be birthed in our individual hearts before it can happen anywhere else. Until our own heart is raised to life, we can't carry the resurrection and healing power of Jesus into the world. Until we know *Love* and accept His love for ourselves, we can't possibly show His love to others.

A CELEBRATION

As the bride of Jesus we have something to celebrate: eternity with our *Husband! Then he said to me, "Write: 'Blessed are those who are called to the marriage supper of the Lamb!'" And he said to me, "These are the true sayings of God" (Revelation 19:7-9).*

We will be *blessed* in the presence of God. It will finally be the big day we've been waiting for. Gathered for the wedding of all weddings and the celebration of all celebrations, we will have overwhelming joy and peace in the presence of *Love.*

When I first started dating my husband He wined and dined me. I had never been delighted in, pursued, or treated with the respect he had for me. Now that I'm in a love relationship with Jesus, He wines and dines me like no other. The ways He delights, pursues, and loves are endless.

Recently Carole and I were out late editing parts of this book. Leaving a little 24hr coffee shop in downtown Charlotte late at night, we were starving. It was too late (we thought) on a weeknight to find anything decent to eat. We figured we may have to eat fast food which neither of us really wanted. Not being familiar with the area we prayed, "Lord, we're so tired and need food. Would you please take us where You want us to go for dinner? Will You direct our steps and help us find something healthy to eat at this late hour? We know nothing is too hard for You."

We drove around in uptown seeing signs for restaurants. Unsure of what was open or available we decided to park in a parking deck and walk to find something. We parked on the bottom level close to the road. That was the first miracle. Straight up a flight of stairs, we ended up in this hidden, beautiful spot, filled with Christmas lights and rows of restaurants. There were numerous eating places still open and they all looked swanky. We were concerned about our budget but figured we were so hungry money didn't matter. We went in the first place. They were closing in a half hour which gave us time to order. When we got our menus we were pleasantly surprised that the food was reasonably priced. Our food was delicious and everything about that night was lovely.

Carole and I literally went on a date with Jesus near midnight. Almost magical, the whole area was lit up and alive with people and music. The life we saw in the city compared in no way to the life we experienced in our own hearts as we were wined and dined by *Love*. He took care of us in every way. When we give our lives to Him in the details (even in where to find food in an unfamiliar place at almost eleven at night), our *Husband* delights to delight in us moment by moment.

Jesus extended an invitation to the church of the Laodiceans:

> *As many as I love, I rebuke and chasten. Therefore be zealous and repent. Behold, I stand at the door and knock. If anyone hears My voice and opens the door, I will come in to him and dine with him, and he with Me (3:19-22).*

They were lukewarm. After mentioning His love for them, with mercy He told them to repent. God doesn't tolerate us being lukewarm. He doesn't want us partially committed to a relationship with Him. He wants us all in. He's knocking. He's inviting. All we have to do is repent and live.

If you want to be wined and dined, *Love* is waiting. He's inviting you to come closer, to ease in by His side. He wants to dine with you and delight in you, but He will not force His way in. He's a *Gentleman*. He's waiting for you to allow Him in. He wants to be intimately involved in the details of your life. Open the door to *Love*. There's no love like His. Letting go, letting in, and letting *Love*, you'll never be the same.

THE INVITATION

You've been invited to the wedding of the Century, of *all* Centuries: past, present, and future. The invitation alone is frame-worthy. It is hand-written in a precious and *expensive crimson*. Trimmed with gold overlay and dusted with diamond glitter, your name is at the center of the invitation. Inside are all the details. You've been given a new wardrobe allowance. Covered by *Love,* your dress will be clean and white. Pure and without blemish you will stand in front of your Groom beaming and radiant. At the reception following, you and your Husband will be the center of attention. At His side a seat has been designated just for you. The first dance is yours. Swaying in the arms of *Divine Love,* He sings sweet songs in your ear. Free and alive, you'll live in intimacy forever with the One who created it. With your invitation in hand, will you respond? The time is now.

> *And the Spirit and the bride say, 'Come!' And let him who hears say, "Come!" And let him who thirsts come. Whoever desires, let him take the water of life freely (Revelation 22:17).*

Questions

1. How are you sensing God's delight and pursuit in your current season of life?

2. In what ways are you responding to His invitation to deeper intimacy?

Ask God to draw you close. Ask Him to hold your hand. Ask Him to open your spiritual eyes to see HIm in the ins and outs of your days.

3. Is the Bride ready for her Bridegroom? Are our hearts repentant and purified?

4. What does Isaiah 58 and 61 say about caring for others? How are we investing all we've been given into things with eternal value?

Ask God to light a fire in your heart to know Him, to disciple others, and to care for the needy. Pray specifically that He would break your heart for what breaks His.

5. In Romans 13:11-12, what does Paul say about the current day and how we should be responding? What is revival? Where does it start? What could spiritual revival do for the world? What can we do individually to start a revival?

6. Do you want the fullness of knowing God intimately? Will you open your heart and life to letting the Bridegroom see and know you fully?

Close your eyes and imagine the intimacy of being face to face with Jesus at the end of your days on earth. Think of your favorite creative outlet: use your outlet to express what you've seen while imagining seeing God. (This could be dancing, singing, writing, painting, drawing, cooking a feast, or a million other creative things.) Try to imagine doing the very thing you were created for (or that thing that makes your heart sing) with the One who created it?

For soaking, listen to:

Kari Jobe. "My Beloved" *Kari Jobe*

Epilogue

My prayer is that in some way this book has drawn you closer to *Love*. Every chapter was written in His presence and with His help. Each story and word was carefully chosen to paint a picture of how it looks to have intimacy with God moment by moment. I could've given you a list but that would've been just that--another list. If you're like me you don't need another list of things to do. He invites us to stop doing and just be.

Each of us are in process. We won't be perfected until heaven. I've experienced deeper intimacy with *Love* myself in this process. I've grown by hearing and seeing Him in new ways. I hope you too were challenged to lean closer, to dig deeper, and to rest more in His embrace.

Three years ago God showed me in a dream that I would write a book. Sometimes I pass dreams off, but this one was different. It was so vivid I wrote it down. In the dream Lysa Terkeurst was the spokesperson. She said, "If you don't soon write your book, RW is going to write his before you." RW was a young, local pastor friend of mine. I'm still not sure of the significance of that part of the dream. I certainly didn't care if he wrote a book before me. To be honest I really didn't care if I ever wrote a book. In the dream I saw multiple copies of a book beautifully displayed in a bookstore window. The book cover was white with big, red letters. I wasn't sure whose book I was seeing, my pastor friend's or mine. I couldn't read the title but I could clearly see the colors.

Lysa continued saying, "Remember, your strength is in the histories."

Unsure of what she meant, I turned to see a nurse friend of mine and asked, "Does she mean the History and Physical?" I was thinking about patient charts having a history and physical.

My friend said, "I don't know. I think so."

Now I realize that dream was from God to direct me in and confirm the writing of this book. As I was laying out the design for the cover, I remembered the dream. As I was reading through the pages to proof for the last time, I was reminded and thought, "My strength really *is* in the histories." I'm not a teacher or writer as much as I am a communicator of truth. I love to tell stories of God's faithfulness.

God's been showing and guiding in this process all along. The book He showed me three years ago in my sleep has now come to fruition and I stand amazed. He wows me every single day! All glory to Jesus who is faithful and true, guiding us in everlasting intimacy.

~*Rivera*

Prayer For Salvation

JESUS,

Thank You for loving me no matter what I've done or where I've been. I believe You died on the cross and rose again so I could have life. I ask for forgiveness and thank You for forgiving me. Thank You for saving me. Thank You for letting me rest in Your embrace every moment of every day for the rest of my life. I thank you for making a way for me to spend eternity in heaven with You. I submit my life to You and invite You to be my Leader and Love. Holy Spirit help me hear and be guided by Your voice.

In Jesus' name,

Amen

Sweet friend,

If you prayed this prayer with me, I would love to know. A simple note in my email inbox saying, "I prayed to receive Jesus as my Savior" would bless me. I would be delighted to celebrate with you. Email me: riveradouthit@gmail.com

Much love,

Rivera

Notes

Bryant, A. 1956. *Climbing the Heights: Daily Devotions*. Grand Rapids: Zondervan, 211.

Chan, F. and Yankoski, D. 2008. *Crazy Love*. Colorado Springs, CO 80918 U.S.A.: David C. Cook, 129.

Hayford, J. W. 2002. *New Spirit filled life Bible*. Nashville, TN: Thomas Nelson Bibles.

Henry, M. 2008. *Matthew Henry's commentary on the whole Bible*. Peabody, Mass.: Hendickson Publishers.

Lewis, C. S. 2009. *The weight of glory and other addresses*. Pymble, NSW: HarperCollins e-books.

Lewis, C. S. 2009. *A Grief Observed*. [S.l.]: HarperCollins.

Lewis, C. S. 2002. *The four loves*. [Place of publication not identified]: HarperCollins.

Lewis, C. S. 2004. *Collected letters of C.S. Lewis*. [San Francisco]: HarperSanFrancisco.

Lewis, C. S. and Hooper, W. 1986. *Present concerns*. San Diego: Harcourt Brace Jovanovich. 17-20.

Lewis, C. S. 1997. *Mere* Christianity. London: Fount.

Lubin, G. 2013. The 12 Most Expensive Weddings In History. [online] Available at: http://www.businessinsider.com/most-expensive-weddings-2010-7#1-prince-charles-and-lady-diana-12 [Accessed: 26 Dec 2013].

Merriam-webster.com. 2014. Intimacy - Definition and More from the Free Merriam-Webster Dictionary. [online] Available at: http://www.merriam-webster.com/dictionary/intimacy [Accessed: 6 Jan 2014].

Peterson, E. H. 2008. The Invitation: A Simple Guide to the Bible. Colorado Springs: Navpress.

Ross, S. 2013. Missionary Quotes - Worldwide Missions - Wholesome Words. [online] Available at: http://www.wholesomewords.org/missions/msquotes.html [Accessed: 26 Dec 2013].

Scientificamerican.com. 2013. Feisty Male Fruit Flies Calmed by Females: Scientific American Podcast. [online] Available at: http://www.scientificamerican.com/podcast/episode.cfm?id=feisty-male-fruit-flies-calmed-by-f-13-11-18 [Accessed: 28 Dec 2013].

Spurgeon, C. H. and Reimann, J. 2010. Morning by morning. Grand Rapids, Mich.: Zondervan. Day 194, 353.

Strong, J. and Strong, J. n.d. The new Strong's expanded exhaustive concordance of the Bible.

Tozer, A. W. 2013. The Pursuit of God. Lanham: Start Publishing LLC. 43, 46, 51, 56.

World-science.net. 2013. Now downloadable: "music" of the stars. [online] Available at: http://www.world-science.net/othernews/060809_spheres.htm [Accessed: 26 Dec 2013].

About The Author

On most mornings you can find Rivera Douthit at her country home in North Carolina sipping coffee on her front porch rocker. She is wife to an amazing man and mama to two beautifully creative children. Since she couldn't keep the goldfish alive, she has no pets.

From a wife-beater tank in the morning to heels in the evening, Rivera is poised in various situations with all types of people. She loves relationships (new and old), the arts, and nature, and has a genuine way of seeing God in all of it. Traveling near and far she shares His love and truth with women through speaking engagements.

Rivera's close friends and family say she's genuine, beautifully straightforward, truth-seeking, loyal, after God's heart, exceedingly generous, and desperate for all to know the freedom of Love Himself and to walk in it daily.

Through transparent writing, her zeal is evident for wanting people to know Jesus intimately. Rivera doesn't claim to be a theologian or have all the answers, but she does stand on the Bible as the final Word. She's journeying messily through life just like everyone else, but her greatest desire is to always point people to the only One who matters–Jesus.

IF THIS BOOK TOUCHED YOU, WILL YOU CONSIDER SHARING IT?

- Mention the book in a Facebook post, Twitter update, Pinterest pin, or blog post.
- Recommend this book to those in your small group, classes, workplace, and church. Invite a group of friends to do the Intimacy Bible Study.
- Tweet "I recommend reading #IntimacyBook by @riveradouthit"
- Pick up a copy for someone who would be encouraged or challenged by this message.
- Write a review on amazon.com

Connect

One of Rivera's greatest joys is connecting with her readers. Feel free to visit her and/or subscribe to her weekly writings at www.riveradouthit.com.

- Send her an email: riveradouthit@gmail.com
- Connect on Instagram @riveradouthit
- Connect on Twitter @riveradouthit #IntimacyBook

28607363R00131

Made in the USA
Columbia, SC
26 October 2018